NEW DIRECTIONS FOR CHILD DEVELOPMENT

William Damon, *Brown University*
EDITOR-IN-CHIEF

Beyond the Parent: The Role of Other Adults in Children's Lives

Robert C. Pianta
University of Virginia

EDITOR

Number 57, Fall 1992

JOSSEY-BASS PUBLISHERS
San Francisco

BEYOND THE PARENT: THE ROLE OF OTHER ADULTS IN CHILDREN'S LIVES
Robert C. Pianta (ed.)
New Directions for Child Development, no. 57
William Damon, Editor-in-Chief

Microfilm copies of issues and articles are available in 16mm and 35mm, as well as microfiche in 105mm, through University Microfilms Inc., 300 North Zeeb Road, Ann Arbor, Michigan 48106.

LC 85-644581   ISSN 0195-2269   ISBN 1-55542-732-4

NEW DIRECTIONS FOR CHILD DEVELOPMENT is part of The Jossey-Bass Education Series and is published quarterly by Jossey-Bass Inc., Publishers, 350 Sansome Street, San Francisco, California 94104-1310 (publication number USPS 494-090). Second-class postage paid at San Francisco, California, and at additional mailing offices. POSTMASTER: Send address changes to Jossey-Bass Inc., Publishers, 350 Sansome Street, San Francisco, California 94104-1310.

EDITORIAL CORRESPONDENCE should be sent to the Editor-in-Chief, William Damon, Department of Education, Box 1938, Brown University, Providence, Rhode Island 02912.

Cover photograph by Wernher Krutein/PHOTOVAULT © 1990.

The paper used in this journal is acid-free and meets the strictest guidelines in the United States for recycled paper (50 percent recycled waste, including 10 percent post-consumer waste). Manufactured in the United States of America.

CONTENTS

Editor's Notes

The origins of this book lie in my experiences as a teacher, through which I learned firsthand the importance of teacher-child relationships. As a teacher in a middle-school special education resource classroom, I had the opportunity to work with the same group of students over the course of two, sometimes three years. During this time, I was counselor, instructor, role model, mentor, and psychological parent; I observed other teachers who filled these roles as well. It became apparent that the students' performance was related to my sense of closeness with them and their sense of security with me. At the time, I had only a sketchy framework within which to understand my experiences; only later at the University of Minnesota did I come to understand the implications of these experiences. This volume is in part a result of that process.

The goal of this volume, *Beyond the Parent: The Role of Other Adults in Children's Lives,* is to provide a framework, or platform, for inquiry into the role of relationships between children and nonparental adults in development. The questions raised and addressed by research on children's relationships with teachers and child care providers are complex. Each chapter is related to an important developmental question: What types of continuity/coherence exist in relationships across people, contexts, roles, and time, and how do children organize their experiences in these relationships despite the inevitable (and necessary) differences that exist? Secondarily, each chapter has implications for policy and practice in child care and school settings.

Van IJzendoorn, Sagi, and Lambermon open the volume with a theory-driven chapter on the conditions under which child-caregiver relationships can be considered attachments. They draw heavily on Bowlby's original work for their hypotheses, then they test these formulations against two samples of data from Holland and Israel in which children were raised with professional caregivers but within widely different caregiving arrangements. The results support the view that child-caregiver relationships include attachments, and the chapter provides important insights on how children organize their relationships with the different adults who provide them with care.

In Chapter Two, Howes and Matheson integrate attachment theory with ecological-cultural analysis to identify contextual factors related to concordance in child-mother and child-caregiver attachments. They provide a rich description of the caregiving interactions that fall under the umbrellas of "home-care" and "day-care" arrangements, and of the wide variety of contexts in which children are actually provided care. A major contribution of the Howes and Matheson chapter is that it illuminates how the question of concordance is affected by family status, child care setting, security of child-mother and child-caregiver attachments, and number of hours in each setting. The question of concordance is not easily reduced to a two-way contingency table. Finally, Howes and Matheson also tackle the question of whether attachment to child care providers can be compensatory, again addressing the issue of how children organize multiple relationships.

In Chapter Three, Hamilton and Howes offer another look at relationships between children and child care providers, contrasting these with child-mother relationships in an attempt to identify behavioral patterns within and across types of relationships. Based on a large sample of children in child care, Hamilton and Howes's chapter suggests that the demands of two different settings (home, child care) produce relationships with children that differ on dimensions such as affective sharing and approach under distress. The data raise interesting questions about how the child functions within two different relationships and about interactions between setting and relationship type.

In Chapter Four, Pianta and Steinberg present data on kindergarten teachers' reports on their relationships with each of the children in their classrooms in a given year. The data illustrate that relationships between children and teachers are based on, but not solely defined by, the children's classroom behavior and are highly predictive of classroom behavior in first grade. The dimensions along which teachers' perceptions of their relationships with children differ are similar to dimensions identified in child-parent relationships. Pianta and Steinberg's data suggest that relationships with children also play a role in teachers' decisions to refer children for retention in kindergarten and may be a protective factor for some children; cases in which children were predicted to be retained but were promoted had more positive relationships with teachers than did those who were retained.

In Chapter Five, Lynch and Cicchetti extend the study of child-teacher relationships by examining maltreated children's perceptions of their relatedness with teachers. The authors clearly describe the importance of studying child-teacher relationships in a sample of maltreated children; such an approach extends theory on normal developmental processes and highlights the protective role that teacher-child relationships may play in normal and deviant development. The data presented by Lynch and Cicchetti indicate that the construct of relatedness is clearly applicable to the child-teacher relationship, and that maltreated childrens' perceptions of and relationships with teachers are consistent with their history of inadequate care, which suggests the possibility that their representational models of self and other are not closed but rather open to new relationship experiences. Finally, Lynch and Cicchetti's data raise important questions about the role of self-system processes and internal representations as mechanisms of continuity across relationships and across time.

In Chapter Six, Kontos provides a cogent review of the preceding chapters from the perspectives of continuity and context. And, in the final chapter, I identify common themes and issues raised by the research presented in the volume and suggest directions for future work. These themes include the complexity of research on relationships across people, contexts, and time, the conditions under which relationships between children and nonparental adults can be considered attachments, the implications of research on these relationships for attachment theory, the implications of relationship concordance for internal working models of the self and other, and a range of problems related to measurement of relationships.

It is my hope that this volume is a stimulus for integrating research on social development with the pressing need for new perspectives on applied problems. Large numbers of children come to school with inadequate relationship histories, and wider networks of caregivers now provide care once confined to smaller, familial systems.

I thank Robert McNergney, director of the Commonwealth Center for the Education of Teachers, for his vision in support of my research on teacher-child relationships; Jeanne Stovall for her efforts in compiling a book manuscript from divergent sources (and diskettes), and, most important, the sixth- and seventh-grade students who demonstrated to me that relationships with teachers were an important influence in their development.

Robert C. Pianta
Editor

ROBERT C. PIANTA is associate professor of school and clinical psychology, Curry School of Education, University of Virginia, Charlottesville. He is associate editor of Early Education and Development and advisory editor for the Journal of School Psychology. His interests in developmental psychopathology involve research on relationships between children and adults, especially the role of relationships in the regulation of behavior and development of psychopathology, and in the applications of research on social development to the process of schooling.

In a multiple caretaker environment, nonparental caregivers can be important attachment figures with considerable impact on children's later socioemotional development.

The Multiple Caretaker Paradox: Data from Holland and Israel

Marinus H. van IJzendoorn, Abraham Sagi, Mirjam W. E. Lambermon

Although Bowlby always resisted identifying the "mother figure" with the child's biological mother and emphasized the possibility of other caregivers—such as fathers or grandmothers—serving as attachment figures, there are two reasons to believe that he considered mothers in Western societies as the principal attachment figures. First, he was convinced that only a stable relationship with regularly recurring interaction episodes could lead to a harmonious "match" between both partners. His "law of continuity" implies that "the more stable and predictable the regime, the more secure a child's attachment tends to be; the more discontinuous and unpredictable the regime, the more anxious his attachment" (Bowlby, 1975, p. 261). In Western societies, the biological mother is more likely to create this condition of continuity. Second, Bowlby was convinced that babies and young children (below three years) are unable to preserve internal representations of the caregivers' availability in their absence; children will be confident about their attachment figures' availability only when they are actually present (Bowlby, 1975, p. 237). Therefore, his "law of accumulated separation experiences" states that "effects of separations from mother during the early

Preparation of this chapter was supported by a Pioneer Grant from the Netherlands Organization for Scientific Research and by a grant from the Scheidegger Corporation to Marinus H. van IJzendoorn. Parts of this chapter were presented at the biennial meeting of the Society for Research in Child Development, Seattle, Washington, April 17–20, 1991. The authors thank M. Bakermans-Kranenburg, K. Haak, H. Zwart-Woudstra, A. van Busschbach, and W. Visser for their assistance in data collection and analysis.

years are cumulative and . . . the safest dose is therefore a zero dose" (Bowlby, 1975, p. 255). It is once again in Western societies that the biological mother is more likely to have the opportunity to be permanently available to the young child.

Monotropy

Against this background, the concept of "monotropy" appears to be a logical implication of fundamental ideas in attachment theory. Literally interpreted, the Greek word *monotropy* means being fed or raised by only one person, that is, the mother. Nevertheless, the concept of monotropy does not seem to fit well into recent developments in attachment theory and practice. First, in present-day Western societies, permanent availability of one and the same attachment figure does not occur in the majority of families in which often more than one child is raised, and in which the parent has to fulfill other responsibilities than just child rearing, often because of economic necessity. Under such circumstances, Bowlby's law of continuity may have to be reformulated to imply the constant availability of an attachment figure, whoever the particular person is. If the child is part of a network of attachment figures, separation from one attachment figure, such as the mother, may not mean separation from every secure base; on the contrary, a separation from the mother during part of the day may imply the presence of the father or a professional caregiver to fulfill the role of attachment figure (Van IJzendoorn and Tavecchio, 1987).

At the same time, a multiple caretaker arrangement does not necessarily mean that children relate to more than one figure in a way that may be called "attachment." Morelli and Tronick (1991), for example, observed that Efe infants (Pygmies from Zaire, Africa) develop primary attachments to their mothers by twelve months of age in the context of experiencing sensitive multiple caregiving during the first year of life. One of the factors determining the development of monotropy within an extended child-rearing arrangement is supposed to be the care at night: infants are cared for solely by their mothers during the night and sleep is interrupted by bouts of social interaction exclusively between mother and infant. The importance of the sleeping arrangement has been made clear in a recent study on home-based and communal kibbutzim (Sagi and others, 1992). The communal sleeping arrangement appeared to be somewhat detrimental to the security of infant-mother attachment as compared to the home-based arrangement in which the infants sleep at home. If mothers take care of their children at night, it may set the groundwork for a special and primary attachment relationship to develop, whatever other caregivers are involved in raising the children during the daytime.

Multiple Caretaker Paradox

The only nonmaternal caregiver who has been studied extensively in the past decade is the father figure (see Fox, Kimmerly, and Schafer, 1991, for a metanalysis on mother-father studies). From these studies, it cannot be derived that fathers are able to establish an attachment relationship equivalent to the infant-mother attachment in every respect. For example, it was concluded that, together, infant-mother and infant-father attachments were more powerful in predicting the child's concurrent behavior than was the infant-mother relationship alone (Main and Weston, 1981; Main, Kaplan, and Cassidy, 1985). In the long term, however, infant-mother attachment appeared to be a better predictor of attachment at six years of age (Main, Kaplan, and Cassidy, 1985). Main and her colleagues suggested that a hierarchy of internal working models of attachment exists in which the mother stands foremost and the father is represented as a subsidiary attachment figure. Indeed, Lamb (1977, 1978) showed that young infants prefer their mothers when distressed, even though most are clearly attached to both parents.

Studies on attachment between infants and professional caregivers are even more scarce (Krentz, 1983). One of the most salient and highly replicated findings is that the quality of attachment relationships with different caretakers is often discordant. The discordance of secure, resistant, and avoidant patterns with respect to father and to mother has been shown by Lamb (1977), Main and Weston (1981), Grossmann, Grossmann, Huber, and Wartner (1981) and Sagi and others (1985). The same lack of concordance of attachment quality within a broader network of infant-caretaker relationships was found in Sagi and others (1985), Goossens and Van IJzendoorn (1990), and Krentz (1983) for infant-parent and infant-professional caregiver relationships. The implications of this basic finding of discordance are far-reaching. Because the infant-mother attachment can predict later socioemotional functioning, an intriguing issue is whether discordant relationships with nonmaternal caretakers can have the same predictive power. If the infant-mother attachment relationship is secure and therefore predicts positive peer interactions (Sroufe, Fox, and Pancake, 1983), what influence may in that case be left for an insecure infant-caregiver relationship? It is hardly imaginable that the same child's insecure relationship with a nonmaternal caregiver would have the opposite effect, that is, would stimulate negative peer interactions. But it is also difficult to imagine that the effect would be positive.

Attachment research can follow at least two different strategies to address the multiple caretaker paradox. First, one may doubt the validity of the nonmaternal attachment measures; more radically, it may even be doubted whether a real attachment relationship can exist between an infant and a nonmaternal caretaker. The Strange Situation procedure as well as its derivative measures, such as the Attachment Q-Sort, are validated against home observations of mother-infant interactions, and there are few data on the validity of these measures for relationships with other caretakers. Moreover, these instruments might assess aspects of the child-caretaker relationship other than attachment. Second, presupposing the existence of infant attachment to nonmaternal caretakers, one may ask how the child internally organizes different attachment relationships. Infant-mother attachment classifications do not predict later socioemotional development exhaustively; in fact, associations with security of the infant-mother relationship are only modest. If children integrate their attachment experiences with different caretakers, later socioemotional development may be better predicted on basis of the quality of the attachment network than through the quality of the infant-mother attachment alone.

In this chapter, we address two questions involved in the multiple caretaker paradox: Do infant-nonmaternal caregiver attachment relationships exist, and, if so, how are multiple attachments interrelated? In trying to answer both questions, we focus on infants' relationships with nonparental caregivers.

Do Infant-Caregiver Attachment Relationships Exist?

To answer this important question, we need criteria to evaluate whether a relationship is correctly identified as an attachment relationship. Bowlby's (1984, p. 371) definition of attachment may imply some of these criteria: "To say of a child that he is attached to, or has an attachment to, someone means that he is strongly disposed to seek proximity to and contact with a specific figure and to do so in certain situations, notably when he is frightened, tired or ill." From this definition, it may be derived that in a stressful circumstance such as the Strange Situation infants should show differential attachment behavior to their professional caregiver compared to a stranger. In the Ainsworth, Blehar, Waters, and Wall (1978) coding system, secure and ambivalent children are discriminated from avoidant children on basis of interactive behavior toward the stranger and the attachment figure. Secure and ambivalent children should distinguish between their attachment figure and an unknown person; in the Strange Situation, avoidant children will not necessarily make this distinction. If a relationship with a professional caregiver can be considered an attachment relationship, we should not find an overrepresentation of attachments classified as avoidant in professional caregiver samples. Differential behavior toward stranger and caregiver indicates secure and ambivalent relationships to be attachment relationships—according to Bowlby's definition and the coding system. In case of child-caregiver relationships classified as avoidant, it is unknown whether the relationship is a truly avoidant attachment or does not contain elements of attachment.

Furthermore, we would expect that infant-caregiver relationships can at least be considered classifiable according to the established coding system, because classifiability would mean that a restricted number of coherent strategies for dealing with the stressful situation are being detected (Main, 1990). In case of unclassifiable infant-caregiver relationships, we should doubt the existence of an attachment in the usual sense. An overrepresentation of unclassifiable cases may throw doubt on the existence of a coherent infant-caregiver attachment strategy to deal with stressful situations.

When infant-caregiver interactions during the Strange Situation are classified as attachments, discordance with the infant-parent attachment classification is to be expected. Because attachment is considered a unique reflection of the dyad's history of interactions, the infant-caregiver classification is required to be independent from other attachment relationships that the child has developed.

Another set of criteria for identifying infant-caretaker attachment relationships may be derived from our expectations about external correlates of Strange Situation classifications. We expect infant-mother classifications to be predicted by maternal sensitivity and to be predictive of later socioemotional development (Ainsworth, Blehar, Waters, and Wall, 1978; Sroufe, Fox, and Pancake, 1983). Therefore, infant-caregiver classifications should also be predicted by the caregiver's sensitivity—in the day-care setting or in the laboratory. Sensitivity to infant's signals should lead to secure attachments, whereas insensitive interactions should predict insecure attachments. Furthermore, infant-caregiver classifications should have predictive validity. Secure attachments should be related to more optimal socioemotional functioning in toddlerhood or kindergarten age, whereas anxious infant-caregiver attachments should lead to less optimal functioning. The predictive validity may be domain-specific, and especially present in out-of-home contexts.

In sum, we have derived five criteria to test whether infant-caregiver relationships are correctly identified as attachment relationships: (1) Infant-caregiver samples do not show an overrepresentation of avoidant classifications. (2) Infant-caregiver samples do not show an overrepresentation of unclassifiable cases. (3) Infant-caregiver classifications are independent of infant-parent classifications. (4) Caregiver's sensitivity is related to the infant-caregiver Strange Situation classifications. (5) Infant-caregiver classifications predict later socioemotional functioning.

How Are Multiple Attachments Interrelated?

When a child grows up in an extended child-rearing environment and has to deal intensively with multiple caretakers, the issue of the relations among multiple attachments becomes important. Four models may be suggested to describe this issue. In the context of Dutch dual-earner families or Israeli kibbutz children, at least three caretakers are involved in raising the children: mother, father, and professional caregiver. The first model is *monotropy* (Bowlby, 1951). As already shown, this model implies that only one figure—mostly the mother—is an important attachment figure, and the influence of other caretakers is marginal, at least in terms of attachment. The second model is *hierarchy* (Bowlby, 1984). As discussed before, in this model, one caretaker—again, mostly the mother—is the most important attachment figure, but other caretakers may be considered subsidiary attachment figures who may serve as a secure base in case the principal attachment figure is not available. The third model is *independence*. This model implies that a child may be attached similarly to several different caretakers, but the attachment relationships may be functional only in those domains in which the child and a specific caretaker have been interacting over a long period of time. Each caretaker specializes in a certain domain, and only in that domain the bond with the child is effective as a secure base. The fourth model is *integration*. In case of a network of three attachment relationships, secure attachments may compensate for insecure attachments. The child would be optimally functioning in a network of three secure relationships, but two secure relationships would be better than one, and the child would be worst off if the attachment network only consists of insecure relationships.

From the monotropy model, we may derive the prediction that only the infant-mother attachment is related to later socioemotional functioning. Other caregivers are unimportant and ineffective in determining children's development. From the hierarchy model, the prediction may be derived that the infant-mother attachment relationship is the most powerful determinant of children's socioemotional development but not the only factor involved. Other attachments may also be predictive in a weaker sense, independently of the specific developmental domain. The independence model may suggest that children's attachments to all three caretakers are equally important in determining later socioemotional functioning, but different caretakers influence different aspects of children's development, depending on their "specialization." Last, the integration model proposes that the most powerful predictor of later socioemotional development involves the quality of the entire attachment network. In this view, attachments of the same child with different attachment figures influence each other. The role of professional caregivers is emphasized by predicting that the extended attachment network is more strongly related to later socioemotional functioning than is the family attachment network containing only parental attachments.

Because similar studies on infant-caregiver attachment relationships were carried out in Israel and Holland, we combined evidence from these studies in our research on the multiple caretaker paradox. The combination of studies has two distinctive advantages. First, conclusions may be based on a firmer empirical foundation; second, crosscultural variations in our data may lead to new insights into the potentials and limits of the role of the nonparental caregiver in children's development.

Procedures of Our Studies

The Dutch and Israeli studies on professional caregivers have similar designs. Both studies are longitudinal: Initial measurements took place when the children were one to two years old; in Holland, the follow-up took place two years later, whereas in Israel they were completed at five years of age. Fathers, mothers, and professional caregivers were involved in both studies; they participated in the Strange Situation procedure with the infants in their care. Both studies included similar follow-up measures for socioemotional and cognitive functioning.

Dutch Study. Eighty children, along with their mothers, fathers, and professional caregivers, served as subjects in this study. The children were all healthy and born at full term, and all families were intact, dual-earner families from a middle-class background. The children were twelve months of age. Five families excluded from an earlier report because the mothers worked less than fifteen hours per week (Goossens and Van IJzendoorn, 1990) were included in the follow-up study. At the second session, about two years later, sixty-eight children with their parents and professional caregivers participated. Families not participating in the follow-up did not differ in socioeconomic status, parental sensitivity, or quality of attachment from those who did participate.

At the first assessment, infants were observed in the Strange Situation procedure and in a free-play session with their three caregivers separately, in counterbalanced order (see Goossens and Van IJzendoorn, 1990, for details). At the second session, children were again invited to our laboratory twice: once with their mother and once with their father, in a counterbalanced order. During this second series of visits, the California Child Q-Sort (CCQ; Block and Block, 1980; Van Lieshout and others, 1983) and the McCarthy Developmental Scales (MDS; Van der Meulen and Smrkovsky, 1985) were completed (as well as some other measures not reported on here). Preschool teachers were asked to complete the Preschool Behavior Inventory (PSBI; Hess, 1966), and the experimenters completed a readiness-to-interact scale. The CCQ is designed to measure ego resilience, ego control, and field independence. Resilience is defined as the competence to react flexibly but also persistently in problem situations. Control is interpreted as the disposition to express impulses and emotions. Field independence is a cognitive style that implies relative absence of distraction by irrelevant features of the problem situation (Block and Block, 1980). The MDS measures cognitive competence and yields a developmental quotient (DQ). The PSBI is designed to measure children's social behavior in terms of independence, aggression, social-verbal competence, and timidity. The readiness-to-interact scale is a rating scale that measures the degree to which the children are ready and willing to interact with an unknown experimenter during the first few minutes of their initial encounters. Reliability of all measures was satisfactory.

Israeli Study. Eighty-six infants were involved in the first assessments at eleven to fourteen months of age. They were observed in the Strange Situation procedure together with their mothers, fathers, and professional caregivers (metaplot). They belonged to fifteen kibbutzim in the northern part of Israel, seven kibbutzim from the United Kibbutz Movement (Takam), and eight kibbutzim from the Arzi movement (Sagi and others, 1985). At the second session, about three and one-half years later, fifty-nine children were retested. Thirty metaplot and thirty kindergarten teachers provided descriptions of the children included in the follow-up. Children not participating in the follow-up (because of technical constraints) did not differ from the original group on distribution of attachment classifications (Oppenheim, Sagi, and Lamb, 1988).

At the first assessment, infants were observed in the Strange Situation procedure with their three caregivers separately, and in a counterbalanced order. The kibbutz early child care coordinators completed questionnaires containing items on the interaction history of child and metapelet; the metapelet's own parental status, experience, training, and desire for the job; and other variables related to the parents (see Sagi and others, 1985, for details). At the second assessment, children were observed in their own living quarters with the Peer Play Scale (PPS; Howes, 1980). Also, the following tests were administered: Kagan Parent Role Test (KPRT; Kagan and Lemkin, 1960), WPSSI IQ test (Lieblich, 1974), Interpersonal Awareness Test (IAT; Borke, 1971), and Stanford Preschool Internal-External Scale (SPIES; Mischel, Zeiss, and Zeiss, 1974). Kindergarten teachers and metaplot completed the CCQ (Block and Block, 1980) and the Preschool Behavior Q-Sort (PBQ; Baumrind, 1968, 1971), respectively. The PPS measures six different levels of play, for example, parallel play and reciprocal play. The KPRT was used to assess the subjects' perceptions of their parents in terms of punitiveness, nurturance, and salience. The WPSSI tests intelligence and generates an IQ index. The IAT was used to assess the child's empathy, operationally defined as the ability to perceive the feelings of another child. The SPIES is a measure for locus of control. The PBQ was designed to assess interpersonal behavior in terms of friendliness, cooperativeness, tractability, submissiveness, goal directedness, achievement orientation, and independence (see Oppenheim, Sagi, and Lamb, 1988, for details on those measures). All measures showed a satisfactory reliability.

It is important to note that for both the Dutch and Israeli studies, professional caregivers involved in the first assessment were different from those involved in the second assessment. In Holland, most day-care centers have a policy of changing caregiver and group at around the age of one and one-half years, and in Israeli kibbutzim, children are routinely assigned to new metaplot when they move from infancy to toddlerhood.

Results and Discussion

In the following sections we present results from the analysis of the Dutch and Israeli data sets regarding the validity of infant-caregiver attachments and the organization of multiple attachments.

Do Infant-Caregiver Attachment Relationships Exist? To evaluate the validity of infant-caregiver Strange Situation classifications, we described five criteria: (1) Infant-caregiver samples should not show an overrepresentation of avoidant classifications. (2) Infant-caregiver samples should not show an overrepresentation of unclassifiable cases. (3) Infant-caregiver classifications are independent of infant-parent classifications. (4) Caregiver's sensitivity is related to the infant-caregiver classifications. And (5) infant-caregiver classifications predict later socioemotional functioning.

In Table 1.1, the percentage distributions of infant-caregiver and infant-parent classifications for both the Dutch and Israeli subjects are presented. From this table, it can be seen that there are only small differences in percentages between avoidant classifications in the three subsamples for both countries, and that there is only a slight overrepresentation of unclassifiable cases for the caregivers in the Dutch sample, but not in the Israeli sample. Furthermore, in earlier reports, we showed that the classifications to the caregiver and to the mother were not related, nor were the classifications to the caregiver and to the father for the Dutch sample (Sagi and others, 1985; Goossens and Van IJzendoorn, 1990). In the Dutch case, the concordance between the infant's attachment classifications to both parents was even significantly stronger than the association between infant-caregiver and infant-parent attachment classifications. In their metanalysis Fox, Kimmerly, and Schafer (1991) found a weak but significant association between infant-mother and infant-father classifications. This may be explained by parents modeling each other's caregiving strategies. Professional caregivers have less opportunity to model parental interactions with the infant.

In searching for determinants of infant-caregiver attachment security, Goossens and Van IJzendoorn (1990) found caregivers of secure

Table 1.1. Percentage Distributions of Infant-Caregiver and Infant-Parent Attachment Classifications in the Dutch and Israeli Samples

	Holland			Israel		
Attachment Classifications	Caregiver (N = 75)	Mother (N = 75)	Father (N = 75)	Caregiver (N = 58)	Mother (N = 56)	Father (N = 55)
Avoidant	28	21	31	12	7	11
Secure	57	68	64	50	54	65
Ambivalent	8	9	4	38	39	24
Unclassified	7	1	1			

Source: Adapted from Goossens and Van Ijzendoorn, 1990; and Oppenheim, Sagi, and Lamb, 1988.

infants to be more sensitive to infants' signals during free play as compared to caregivers with whom infants had developed anxious attachment relationships. In a small study on thirty professional caregivers, we
found evidence that sensitivity measured in a free-play session in the
laboratory correlates with sensitivity in a day-care group (Oosterwijk
and Reitsma, 1986). Because the caregiver's sensitivity was not included
in the Israeli study, this validity issue still begs for further examination in
the Israeli case. Indirect evidence is suggestive though, from the following metaplot data.

Our fifth criterion states that infant-caregiver classification should
predict children's later socioemotional functioning. In the Dutch study,
we performed a discriminant function analysis using the PSBI scales for
Independence, Timidity, Aggressiveness, and Social-Verbal Competence,
and a readiness-to-interact scale as "predictors" of avoidant, resistant,
and secure attachment to the caregiver. Because sex of child has been
shown to make a difference in terms of social competence in preschool
(Zaslow and Hayes, 1986), we controlled for sex of child. Furthermore,
to show whether infant-caregiver attachment is uniquely related to the
social competence variables, we also controlled for quality of the attachment network in the family. Sex of child and quality of the attachment
network were introduced first into the hierarchical discriminant function, and the social competence variables were introduced in a second
step. In Table 1.2, the results of this discriminant function analysis are
presented. From this table, it can be derived that avoidant children are
more aggressive and more independent in preschool, and less ready to
interact with a stranger than are children who were securely attached to
their professional caregivers in their second year of life. Resistant children tended to be somewhat more aggressive than secure or avoidant
children.

In the Israeli study, multivariate analyses of variance were used to
determine whether children classified in the secure group with their
metaplot differed from ambivalent children on the peer play, parent-role
perception, empathy, and locus-of-control dependent measures (Oppenheim, Sagi, and Lamb, 1988). Too few avoidant infant-caregiver
classifications were involved to allow for separate analyses on the two
insecure groups. Three out of four multivariate analyses revealed significant differences between the secure and ambivalent children. Children
classified as secure with their metaplot were more empathic, dominant,
purposive, achievement-oriented, and independent than were the ambivalent children. They were also significantly more ego undercontrolled
than the ambivalent subjects (Oppenheim, Sagi, and Lamb, 1988). All of
these differences were in the direction predicted on the basis of prior
attachment research on mothers (Erickson, Sroufe, and Egeland, 1985;
Van IJzendoorn, Van der Veer, and Van Vliet-Visser, 1987). Therefore,

Table 1.2. Results of Discriminant Function Analysis of Social Competence Variables

Social Competence	Avoidant M (N = 14)	Secure M (N = 33)	Resistant M (N = 9)	Correlations of Predictors with Discriminant Functions 1	2	Univariate F(2,35)
Independence[a]	10.8	9.5	9.8	.60	—	2.7
Sex[a]	1.7	1.4	1.3	.45	.43	2.2
Readiness[a]	43.6	50.9	47.8	-.40	—	1.2
Social-verbal	13.6	13.0	12.0	—	—	1.0
Family attitude[a]	2.3	2.3	1.9	—	.54	1.2
Aggressiveness[a]	5.3	4.6	5.9	.32	-.49	1.7
Timidity	5.5	6.0	6.3	—	—	.4

[a] p < .05

these findings lend some support to the predictive validity of the attachment classifications involving kibbutz-reared Israeli infants with their metaplot.

According to our five criteria for evaluating the validity of infant-caregiver Strange Situation classifications, we have reason to believe that children are able to develop an attachment relationship to their professional caregivers. Infant-caregiver samples do not show an overrepresentation of avoidant classifications, and the number of unclassifiable cases is very limited. Furthermore, infant-caregiver classifications do not appear to be simple copies of infant-parent classifications; they seem to reflect the caregiver-infant interaction history in terms of sensitivity; and, last, infant-caregiver classifications are related to children's later socioemotional functioning. Of course, this conclusion depends on the specific child-rearing arrangements in Israeli kibbutzim or in Dutch dual-earner families. In both cases, the professional caregivers had been intensively involved in rearing the infant from at least three months prior to the first Strange Situation measurements. In both cases, the quality of the care provided is relatively high (Goossens and Van IJzendoorn, 1990; Sagi and others, 1985), and the infants were born in well-educated, predominantly middle-class families.

Furthermore, we should also qualify our tentative conclusion that the infant-caregiver relationship really is an attachment relationship. First, the correlational design of our studies precludes definite conclusions about cause and effect (Lamb, Thompson, Gardner, and Charnov, 1985). Second, the bond between caregiver and child is disrupted during the preschool period, in Israel as well as in Holland. The internal representation of a disrupted attachment relationship may have some specific qualities and characteristics different from the representation developed through interactions with stable attachment figures such as parents.

How Are Multiple Attachments Interrelated? We formulated four different models to describe attachment in a multiple caretaker environment: monotropy, hierarchy, independence, and integration. We also derived specific predictions from these models that we tested with our Dutch and Israeli data.

In Table 1.3, data on the different models are presented. We compared the predictive power of infant-mother attachment with that of the family and that of the extended network. Quality of infant-mother attachment was transformed into a continuous scale by assigning numbers to classification types according to the following rule: A and C (1); B4 (2); B1 and B2 (3); B3 (4). This transformation is based on the proposition by Main, Kaplan, and Cassidy (1985) that implies that B1, B2, and B4 receive the same, intermediate security status. We decided to assign the B4 children to a somewhat lower security scale score because of earlier research on this marginal group (Van IJzendoorn, Van der Veer, and Van Vliet-Visser, 1987; Sagi and others, 1985).

Table 1.3. Correlations Between Security of Attachment (Mother, Family Network, Extended Network) and Children's Developmental Status

Children's Development	Holland			Israel		
	Mother	Family	Extended	Mother	Family	Extended
Developmental quotient/Intelligence quotient	-.03	.16	.20[c]	.26	.38[d]	.31[c]
Resilience	-.03	-.06	-.12	-.05	.42[d]	.35[d]
Undercontrol	-.01	.08	.05	.00	.20	.38[d]
Field independence	-.07	-.06	-.14	.08	.41[d]	.34[c]
Hostility[a]	—	—	—	-.11	-.02	-.03
Resistance[a]	—	—	—	-.01	.00	.03
Intractability[a]	—	—	—	.09	.07	.14
Dominance[a]	—	—	—	.15	.23	.31[c]
Goal directed[a]	—	—	—	.04	.36[d]	.47[d]
Achievement[a]	—	—	—	.15	-.02	.16
Independence[a]	—	—	—	.18	.27[c]	.33[c]
Peer play	—	—	—	.02	.06	-.02
Empathy	—	—	—	.04	.20	.34[c]
Locus of control	—	—	—	-.15	-.10	-.15
Sociability[b]	-.02	.00	.02	—	—	—
Timidity[b]	.04	.10	.08	—	—	—
Aggressiveness[b]	.08	-.22	-.14	—	—	—
Independence[b]	.32[d]	.08	.25[c]	—	—	—
Readiness	-.18	-.02	-.11	—	—	—

[a] From the Preschool Behavior Q-Sort of Baumrind, 1968, 1971.
[b] From the Preschool Behavior Inventory of Hess, 1966.
[c] $p < .05$

The quality of the family attachment network was estimated according to the following rule: both attachments insecure (1); one of the attachments insecure and the other attachment secure (2); both attachments secure (3). Finally, the quality of the extended attachment network was computed as follows: three attachments insecure (1); two attachments insecure, one secure (2); one attachment insecure, two attachments secure (3); three attachments secure (4).

In Table 1.3, correlations of these security scales with several measures for children's cognitive and socioemotional development are presented. Because the security scales for mother, mother and father, and mother, father, and professional caregiver are continuous, the sizes of the correlations are comparable. From this table, it can be derived that in the Dutch sample security of extended network was related to the MDS scales for developmental quotient and autonomous behavior in preschool. Infant-mother attachment was only related to autonomous preschool behavior. There were no significant correlations between any of the attachment indices and resilience, undercontrol, or field independence. The predictive power of the extended attachment network is somewhat better than that of the family attachment network and of the separate infant-parent attachments.

The predictive power of attachment in the Israeli sample was much more impressive. A secure extended network was related to a higher IQ and to more independent behavior in kindergarten. This result replicates the Dutch data described before. Furthermore, extended network attachment was related to ego resilience, ego control, and field independence, as well as to dominance and goal-directed behavior in kindergarten and to empathy. The direction of these relations is in accordance with previous research results concerning the effects of infant-mother attachment (Sroufe, Fox, and Pancake, 1983; Van IJzendoorn, Van der Veer, and Van Vliet-Visser, 1987); their strength is impressive. The quality of the family attachment network was significantly related to fewer variables (five) than was the extended network (eight). The quality of family network was not related to ego control, dominance, and empathy in kindergarten. Even more remarkable is the complete lack of significant correlations for the quality of infant-mother attachment in the Israeli study.

We also partialed out IQ and DQ scores from our analyses in order to exclude the possibility that children's socioemotional development may be confounded with their IQ or DQ. But partialing IQ or DQ did not change the correlations in significant ways. IQ scores and other outcome measures at age five were independently predicted from quality of attachment as assessed during infancy. Intelligence also was best predicted on basis of quality of attachment networks. These intriguing and replicated findings further support the hypothesis of a relation between attachment and cognition (Bus and Van IJzendoorn, 1988).

The Israeli data do not support the monotropy model at all. Non-maternal caregivers such as father and metaplot may indeed be important attachment figures determining the course of the children's development in their care. There was also little support for the hierarchy model. Against the background of our data, it does not make sense to consider nonmaternal caregivers only as subsidiary attachment figures. The inclusion of fathers and professional caregivers in the prediction of children's development on basis of their earlier attachment experiences increased the predictive power considerably. At least in a kibbutz child-rearing arrangement, and to a lesser extent in Dutch dual-earner families, the hierarchy model neglects the important contribution of nonmaternal caregivers to the children's feelings of security and their development. It is more difficult, however, to evaluate the independence and integration models against our data. Oppenheim, Sagi, and Lamb (1988) seem to support the independence model in stating that the infant-metaplot attachments were related to later social functioning in children's houses and kindergartens. This finding was interpreted as consistent with the fact that metaplot directly socialize children in this out-of-home context on a daily basis. The correlates of kibbutz infant-mother and infant-father relationships were hypothesized to be limited to home and family contexts.

In Table 1.3, however, we presented several significant correlates of the family attachment network in an out-of-home context. These data seem to clarify the earlier interpretation of the independence model. It should be recalled that previous strategies to analyze multiple attachment relationships were inspired by the monotropy model, and therefore every single infant-adult relationship was tested separately. Now, with our new strategy of developing a "network scale," qualitative network assumptions were operationalized in terms of a continuous scale, which has proved useful and revealing. More specifically, we have shown that the combination of infant-mother and infant-father attachments, but not the separate relationships, was predictive of later cognitive and socio-emotional functioning, which may be interpreted as support for the integration model. Addition of the metaplot to the attachment network would in that case lead to even stronger predictions—and Table 1.3 shows this to be the case.

This network approach should be looked upon differently from previous findings in several studies in which it was shown that the quality of attachment relationships with different caretakers was discordant (Lamb, 1977; Main and Weston, 1981; Grossmann, Grossmann, Huber, and Wartner, 1981; Sagi and others, 1985). Although Sagi and others (1985) handled the data in terms of dependence without suggesting implications for the integration of these discordant internal working models (Bretherton, 1985), the network approach can be viewed as a new move toward a more complex consideration of how different internal working models of attachment relationships might integrate and relate to other indices of development.

Of course, we have to qualify the support for the integration model in several ways. First, we found much stronger relations in the Israeli study than in the Dutch study, although the Dutch data do not contradict our conclusions. Procedural differences in these studies may explain the different findings. In the kibbutz study, nonparental caregivers were heavily involved in assessing the children's development at kindergarten age. In the Dutch study, the parents were responsible for assessing the children's ego resilience and control. Although the parental CCQ version has been thoroughly validated in Holland (Van Lieshout and others, 1983), nonparental caregivers may have a somewhat more "objective" perspective on children's functioning in comparison to peers. In the Dutch case, the MDS and the PSBI showed some relation with attachment, and parents were not involved in completing these measures.

Second, crosscultural differences also may account for the differences in outcome between the Dutch and Israeli studies. In the Dutch case, dual-earner families are a relatively new phenomenon. In Holland, the participation rate of mothers of young children in the labor force has been one of the lowest in Europe. We cannot digress on the specific historical reasons for this situation (see Clerkx and Van IJzendoorn, 1992, for a detailed description), but dual-earner families are still considered a minority and generally seen as negative examples of child rearing. The social prejudices against day care may cause stresses on all caregivers involved (not only the parents) and may override the influence of attachment relationships on children's development. In the kibbutz context, nonparental care is, of course, integrated and accepted, and the social context is favorable to this arrangement of an extended network of caretakers. In the "natural laboratory" of the kibbutz, the consequences of shared caretaking may therefore be much more clearcut.

Finally, it should be recalled that the kibbutz sample considered here entirely represented children living in a communal sleeping arrangement. Because the negative influence of sleeping out of home is clear now (Sagi and others, 1992), the importance of the integration model can be more vigorously examined under this unusual circumstance. The situation of being "deprived" at night may leave more room for the influence of a network of attachment relationships relative to that of separate attachment relationships.

Conclusion

The multiple caretaker paradox describes the contradictions involved in the discordance of infants' attachments to different caretakers. How can attachment be predictive of socioemotional development if the child is attached in a different way to different caretakers? Two questions were raised: Are children really attached to nonparental caregivers? And how are multiple attachments interrelated?

In answering the first question, we proposed five criteria to evaluate whether relationships can be characterized as attachments. On the basis of data from a Dutch and an Israeli study of infant-mother, -father, and -caregiver attachments, we concluded that infants may be considered attached to their professional caregiver. It remains unclear, however, in what ways the children digest the "loss" of their professional caregivers, who change on a regular basis. This early loss may make the mental representation of the nonparental attachment different from that of the parental attachment. This loss notwithstanding, the first infant-caregiver attachment appeared to be a strong predictor of later socioemotional development, especially in the Israeli case.

In addressing the second question, we proposed four models of interrelation between multiple attachments: monotropy, hierarchy, independence, and integration. Evaluating these models against our data from Holland and Israel, we found some support for the integration model: In a multiple caretaker environment, it appears to make a difference whether the child has developed none, one, two, or three secure attachments. Children appear to profit most from three secure relationships. If their attachments to their mothers are insecure and their attachments to fathers and professional caregivers secure, however, they are better off compared to the situation in which the insecure infant-mother relationship is not compensated by secure attachments to other caregivers. We emphasized, though, that a definitive choice between the independence and the integration models is difficult to make. Further research with more extensive measures of children's socioemotional development in different situations (home, day care) and in less unusual social environments is needed to find a way out of the multiple caretaker paradox.

References

Ainsworth, M.D.S., Blehar, M. C., Waters, E., and Wall, S. *Patterns of Attachment: A Psychological Study of the Strange Situation.* Hillsdale, N.J.: Erlbaum, 1978.

Baumrind, D. *Manual for the Preschool Behavior Q-Sort.* Berkeley: Department of Psychology, University of California, Berkeley, 1968.

Baumrind, D. "Current Patterns of Parental Authority." *Developmental Psychology Monographs,* 1971, *4* (1, pt. 2).

Block, J. H., and Block, J. "The Role of Ego Control and Ego Resiliency in the Organization of Behavior." In W. A. Collins (ed.), *Development of Cognition, Affect, and Social Relations.* Minnesota Symposia on Child Psychology, vol. 13. Hillsdale, N.J.: Erlbaum, 1980.

Borke, H. "Interpersonal Perception of Young Children: Egocentrism or Empathy?" *Developmental Psychology,* 1971, *5,* 263–269.

Bowlby, J. *Maternal Care and Mental Health.* Geneva, Switzerland: World Health Organization, 1951.

Bowlby, J. *Attachment and Loss.* Vol. 2: *Separation, Anxiety, and Anger.* Harmondsworth, England: Penguin, 1975.

Bowlby, J. *Attachment and Loss.* Vol. 1: *Attachment.* (2nd ed.) London, England: Penguin, 1984.

Bretherton, I. "Attachment Theory: Retrospect and Prospect." In I. Bretherton and E. Waters (eds.), *Growing Points of Attachment: Theory and Research.* Monographs of the Society for Research in Child Development, vol. 50, nos. 1–2 (serial no. 209). Chicago: University of Chicago Press, 1985.

Bus, A. G., and Van IJzendoorn, M. H. "Mother-Child Interactions, Attachment, and Emergent Literacy: A Cross-Sectional Study." *Child Development,* 1988, *59,* 1262–1273.

Clerkx, L. E., and Van IJzendoorn, M. H. "Child Care in a Dutch Context: On the History, Current Status, and Evaluation of Nonmaternal Child Care in the Netherlands." In M. E. Lamb, K. J. Sternberg, C. P. Hwang, and A. G. Broberg (eds.), *Child Care in Context: Crosscultural Perspectives.* Hillsdale, N.J.: Erlbaum, 1992.

Erickson, M. F., Sroufe, L. A., and Egeland, B. "The Relationship Between Quality of Attachment and Behavior Problems in Preschool in a High-Risk Sample." In I. Bretherton and E. Waters (eds.), *Growing Points of Attachment: Theory and Research.* Monographs of the Society for Research in Child Development, vol. 50, nos. 1–2 (serial no. 209). Chicago: University of Chicago Press, 1985.

Fox, N. A., Kimmerly, N. L., and Schafer, W. D. "Attachment to Mother/Attachment to Father: A Meta-Analysis." *Child Development,* 1991, *62,* 210–225.

Goossens, F. A., and Van IJzendoorn, M. H. "Quality of Infants' Attachment to Professional Caregivers: Relation to Infant-Parent Attachment and Daycare Characteristics." *Child Development,* 1990, *61,* 832–837.

Grossmann, K. E., Grossmann, K., Huber, F., and Wartner, U. "German Children's Behavior Towards Their Mothers at 12 Months and Their Fathers at 18 Months in Ainsworth's Strange Situation." *International Journal of Behavioral Development,* 1981, *4,* 157–181.

Hess, R. D. *Techniques for Assessing Cognitive and Social Abilities of Children and Parents in Project Headstart.* Report No. OE0519. Chicago: University of Chicago Press, 1966.

Howes, C. "Peer Play Scale as an Index of Complexity of Peer Interaction." *Developmental Psychology,* 1980, *16,* 371–372.

Kagan, J., and Lemkin, J. "The Child's Differential Perception of Parental Attributes." *Journal of Abnormal and Social Psychology,* 1960, *61,* 440–447.

Krentz, M. S. "Qualitative Differences Between Mother-Child and Caregiver-Child Attachments and Infants in Family Day Care." Paper presented at the biennial meeting of the Society for Research in Child Development, Detroit, Michigan, March 1983.

Lamb, M. E. "Father-Infant and Mother-Infant Interaction in the First Year of Life." *Child Development,* 1977, *48,* 167–181.

Lamb, M. E. "Qualitative Aspects of Mother-Infant and Father-Infant Attachment." *Infant Behavior and Development,* 1978, *1,* 265–275.

Lamb, M. E., Thompson, R. A., Gardner, W. P., and Charnov, E. L. *Infant-Mother Attachment: The Origins and Developmental Significance of Individual Differences in Strange Situation Behavior.* Hillsdale, N.J.: Erlbaum, 1985.

Lieblich, A. *WPPSI Manual.* Jerusalem, Israel: Psychological Corporation, Hebrew University, 1974.

Main, M. "Cross-Cultural Studies of Attachment Organization: Recent Studies, Changing Methodologies, and the Concept of Conditional Strategies." *Human Development,* 1990, *33,* 48–61.

Main, M., and Weston, D. R. "The Quality of the Toddler's Relationship to Mother and to Father: Related to Conflict Behavior and the Readiness to Establish New Relationships." *Child Development,* 1981, *52,* 932–940.

Main, M., Kaplan, N., and Cassidy, J. "Security in Infancy, Childhood, and Adulthood: A Move to the Level of Representation." In I. Bretherton and E. Waters (eds.), *Growing Points of Attachment: Theory and Research.* Monographs of the Society for Research in Child Development, vol. 50, nos. 1–2 (serial no. 209). Chicago: University of Chicago Press, 1985.

Mischel, W., Zeiss, R., and Zeiss, H. "Internal-External Control and Persistence: Validation and Implications of the Stanford Preschool Internal-External Scale." *Journal of Personality and Social Psychology*, 1974, *19*, 265–278.

Morelli, G. A., and Tronick, E. Z. "Efe Multiple Caretaking and Attachment." In J. L. Gewirtz and W. M. Kurtines (eds.), *Intersections with Attachment*. Hillsdale, N.J.: Erlbaum, 1991.

Oosterwijk, T., and Reitsma, J. "Crecheleidsters en hun sensitiviteit" [Sensitivity of day-care providers]. Unpublished master's thesis, Department of Clinical Education, Leiden University, The Netherlands, 1986.

Oppenheim, D., Sagi, A., and Lamb, M. E. "Infant-Adult Attachments in the Kibbutz and Their Relation to Socioemotional Development 4 Years Later." *Developmental Psychology*, 1988, *24*, 427–433.

Sagi, A., and others. "Security of Infant-Mother, -Father, -Metapelet Attachments Among Kibbutz-Reared Israeli Children." In I. Bretherton and E. Waters (eds.), *Growing Points of Attachment: Theory and Research*. Monographs of the Society for Research in Child Development, vol. 50, nos. 1–2 (serial no. 209). Chicago: University of Chicago Press, 1985.

Sagi, A., and others. "Sleeping Out of Home in a Kibbutz Communal Arrangement: It Makes a Difference for Infant-Mother Attachment." Unpublished manuscript, Department of Psychology, Haifa University, Israel, 1992.

Sroufe, L. A., Fox, N.A., and Pancake, V. R. "Attachment and Dependency in Developmental Perspective." *Child Development*, 1983, *54*, 1615–1627.

Van der Meulen, B. F., and Smrkovsky, M. *MOS 2½–8½. McCarthy Ontwikkelingsschalen* [McCarthy Developmental Scales]. Lisse, The Netherlands: Swets and Zeitlinger, 1985.

Van IJzendoorn, M. H., and Tavecchio, L.W.C. "The Development of Attachment Theory as a Lakatosian Research Program: Philosophical and Methodological Aspects." In L.W.C. Tavecchio and M. H. van IJzendoorn (eds.), *Attachment in Social Networks: Contributions to the Bowlby-Ainsworth Attachment Theory*. Amsterdam, The Netherlands: Elsevier Science, North-Holland, 1987.

Van IJzendoorn, M. H., Van der Veer, R., and Van Vliet-Visser, S. "Attachment Three Years Later: Relationships Between Quality of Mother-Infant Attachment and Emotional/Cognitive Development in Kindergarten." In L.W.C. Tavecchio and M. H. van IJzendoorn (eds.), *Attachment in Social Networks: Contributions to the Bowlby-Ainsworth Attachment Theory*. Amsterdam, The Netherlands: Elsevier Science, North-Holland, 1987.

Van Lieshout, C.F.M., and others. *Zelfstandigheidsontwikkeling in het basisonderwijs* [Autonomy in elementary school]. Intern Rapport 83 ON 04, SVO-Project BS560. Nijmegen, The Netherlands, 1983.

Zaslow, M. J., and Hayes, C. D. "Sex Differences in Children's Responses to Psychosocial Stress: Towards a Cross-Context Analysis." In M. E. Lamb, A. L. Brown, and B. Rogoff (eds.), *Advances in Developmental Psychology*. Vol. 4. Hillsdale, N.J.: Erlbaum, 1986.

MARINUS H. VAN IJZENDOORN *is professor of child and family studies at Leiden University, The Netherlands. His research interests concern attachment and methodology.*

ABRAHAM SAGI *is professor of psychology at Haifa University, Israel. His research interests concern attachment and policy issues.*

MIRJAM W. E. LAMBERMON *is interested in research and clinical implications of attachment theory.*

Ecological-cultural analysis of child care and family settings yields insight into factors affecting concordance of child-adult relationships.

Contextual Constraints on the Concordance of Mother-Child and Teacher-Child Relationships

Carollee Howes, Catherine C. Matheson

In attempting to understand children's relationships with their child care teachers, we have drawn on two somewhat disparate theoretical traditions—ecological-cultural theory and attachment theory. Ecological-cultural theory is useful for interpreting the context of relationship formation. Attachment theory provides a developmental framework for understanding relationship formation. Since there is no universal nomenclature to describe the adult who cares for children in child care (he or she may be a family day-care parent or provider, a caregiver, or a teacher), we use the term *teacher* in this chapter to mean any alternative to the parent caregiver.

Ecological-cultural theory proposes that social-ecological influences on children's development occur through activity settings (Weisner, 1984, 1988). The activity setting construct, rather than the individual, becomes the unit of analysis in explaining child development. Activity settings provide a context for social interaction and the formation of relationships. Activity settings are defined by (1) the personnel present, (2) cultural beliefs and values, (3) motives and emotions guiding action, (4) the task involved, and (5) scripts for appropriate conduct (Weisner,

We appreciate the efforts of the research team who worked on the studies reported here: Kristin Droege, Darlene Galluzzo, Annette Groen, Claire Hamilton, Catherine Matheson, Lisabeth Meyers, Jacqueline Moore, Leslie Phillipsen, Ellen Wolpow, and Fang Wu. We are very grateful for the graciousness of the families and child care teachers who allowed us to study the children. Portions of the studies were supported by a grant from the Spencer Foundation.

Reprint requests may be addressed to Carollee Howes, Graduate School of Education, University of California, Los Angeles, CA 90024-1521, U.S.A.

1988). The home environment is composed of a group of activity settings, such as feeding, putting to bed, toileting, and playing games. If, for example, the activity setting is feeding the baby, an activity setting analysis would (1) identify who is present in the setting and who does the task, for example, both parents are present and mother breast-feeds; (2) determine what belief systems led to the practice of breast feeding; (3) observe the emotional tone of the feeding interaction; (4) observe whether there are other tasks in the setting that compete for an adult's attention; and (5) observe the sequence of events involved in feeding the infant. By analyzing activity settings for physical and emotional care of children across child care and home environments, researchers can examine the pervasiveness and emotional salience of each caregiving relationship (Matheson, Rose, and Howes, 1991).

Attachment theory provides an explanation for the child's emotional security with caregivers and for the formation of internal working models of relationships. According to the theory, both the child's felt security with an adult and the child's internal models of relationships are derived from the experience of recurrent interactions with that adult (Bowlby, 1982). Experiences of receiving physical and emotional care from that adult are salient in the formation of attachment relationships. Physical care includes feeding, cleaning, changing, and carrying. Emotional care includes comforting, holding, preparing the child for future, potentially stressful events (such as the doctor's office), helping the child to get to sleep, touching, proximity, and warmth (Matheson, Rose, and Howes, 1991). Both physical care and emotional care are part of the formation of an attachment relationship, although emotional care may be more important for the quality of the relationship (Bowlby, 1982).

Repeated physical and emotional caregiving interactions create a set of expectancies about the caregiver's behavior. The expectancies are based on the child's usual and modal experiences with the caregiver. These expectancies form the basis for the child's internal model of that relationship as either providing or not providing both physical and emotional security (Bretherton, 1985).

Attachment theory suggests that the child's internal working model of the attachment figure becomes abstracted from schemas of specific interactions into general beliefs about caregiver characteristics. These beliefs develop into a theory of self and other that is the child's working model for future relationships. Thus, the child's first attachment relationship is assumed to affect subsequent relationships (Bretherton, 1985; Sroufe, 1988).

All children in European-American cultures, except in the most extreme cases of maternal separation, form attachment relationships with their mothers. However, Bowlby's (1982) early formulation of attachment theory recognized that most infants have more than one adult caregiver and are therefore likely to form multiple attachments. Early research into the existence of attachment relationships by Ainsworth, Bell, and Stayton (1974) and Schaffer and Emerson (1964) and more contemporary research on father-child attachments confirmed that single attachments were the exception, not the rule (Bridges, Connell, and Belsky, 1988).

Attachment theory is more clear about the existence of multiple attachments than it is about the relations among these multiple attachments. Most work conducted within the framework of the theory assumes that the primary attachment serves as the template for other social or intimate relationships (Sroufe and Fleeson, 1988). The mother is usually assumed to be the primary attachment figure due to her primacy and/or emotional saliency. This hierarchical model works best as an explanation when children encounter attachment figures in temporal sequence, as when children enter child care well after their maternal attachment relationships are well established. According to this model, these children's relationships with their child care teachers are concordant with or similar to their maternal attachment relationships.

Matheson, Rose, and Howes (1991) propose an alternative model to account for relations among multiple attachment figures, particularly nonconcordant relations, based on an activity setting approach. This model proposes that attachment relationships are embedded within the particular activities and settings in which a relationship is salient. Within this model, a child's relationship with a teacher would be different from her relationship with her mother if the two caregivers were dissimilar in caregiving activities. The activity setting model appears particularly useful for understanding relations between the teacher and the mother attachment relationships of children who begin child care prior to the establishment of maternal attachment relationships and for children whose caregiving experiences in child care and at home lack continuity.

When children enroll in child care, they have at least two primary activity settings of caregiving. These two activity settings may be extremely different or may be quite similar. However, the two activity settings are likely to differ in emotional intensity. Even caregivers in child care settings who state that their goal is to provide love and become a second mother to the child are observed to be less emotionally attentive than mothers (Eheart and Leavitt, 1989).

In this chapter, we use the activity setting model to examine the concordance of mother and teacher attachment relationships of toddler-age children. The children in our samples experienced a variety of child care arrangements. We describe the various child care settings of children in the sample and compare them to home activity settings. Our argument is that as the child care activity settings become more disparate from the child's home activity settings, there is less concordance between the child's attachment relationships in these two types of settings.

Activity Settings at Home and in Child Care

Activity settings provide a natural unit of analysis for examining relationships between children and adults. In the following sections, we identify interactions and roles within the home and child care settings that may impact adult-child relationships.

Home. The mother-child attachment relationship is formed within the activity settings of the home. Even in dual-career households with egalitarian ideology, the mother is usually the primary home-based caregiver (Weisner and Wilson-Mitchell, 1990). Our Western culture values close mother-child ties, and thus the values and goals of the home activity setting tend to establish a loving mother-child relationship. The tasks of caring for the infant within the home are private, completed either by the mother alone or in the context of the father and a sibling or two. Although mothers vary greatly in their sensitivity and responsiveness, the infant is not usually competing with age-mates for her attention. The identity of the caregiver is predictable and limited to one or two adults. These adults are almost always related to the child and thus have some emotional investment in this particular child.

Family Type. In our samples, we have three subtypes of families. One type is composed of stable two-parent families. During the course of our contact with them, parental employment status and number of siblings did not change, and they did not report any abnormal family stresses. In a second type of family, there was only one parent, usually the mother, and/or the family reported that events such as chronic illness, moving, changing employment, or the addition of a sibling created family stress. We categorized these families as stressed. The final type was composed of disorganized families. These families, all receiving state-subsidized child care, experienced unusual family events, including parental incarceration, homelessness, and suspected child abuse. Life within the family from the child's point of view was sometimes chaotic. Where the child lived and who provided child care were not always predictable. Although we conducted no observations within the homes of children in this sample, we assumed that these three types of families created activity settings that differed in personnel, values, disparity between values and behaviors, emotional intensity, and predictability.

Child Care. Child care settings are highly varied. This analysis focuses on model center care, in-home center care, family day care, and licensing.

Model Center Care. The first child care activity setting in our typology is full-time care in child care centers geared toward enhancement of child development and provision of family support. Within these centers, both the number of adults caring for infants and toddlers and the peer group were kept small and as stable as possible. Children were assigned to caregivers, so the same teacher usually provided the physical care for the child. However, teachers did work in shifts, so unlike within-home activity settings, a child could not depend on having a favorite or assigned caregiver present at all times. In these centers, the teachers received some in-service training and supervision regarding what child development experts consider appropriate care for infants and toddlers. There was, of course, variability in how much these ideas were adopted into caregiving routines. And even in this type of care setting in which individualized care for infants and toddlers is valued, children must compete with age-mates for the attention of the teacher.

A child care center activity setting also differs from a home activity setting in its physical environment. Within a center there are fewer dangerous and therefore prohibited objects than are present within a home. In addition, furniture and equipment are child sized. However, unlike home settings, toys and equipment belong to the group and must be shared.

Within child care center activity settings, the scripts for caregiving must accommodate the entire group of children as well as the individual child. The model centers use rituals and routines to facilitate this group process. For example, in our sample, teachers used the same clapping song day after day to facilitate the wait for everyone to receive snack. Naps and bottles were individualized. That is, not all children went to nap or received bottles at once. However, rituals also accompanied these activity settings. For example, all children were rocked when fed a bottle and all children had their backs rubbed before naps.

In-Home Center Care. Our second child care activity setting is difficult to classify in terms of usual child care forms. It was a small, unlicensed child care center located within a home. Only full-time toddler-age children attended the center. The two teachers were both present all day and thus the personnel of the center were stable and predictably present much as in a home activity setting. These teachers were not trained in child development, yet they had evolved a strong and consistent set of values and practices for providing child care. Parents warmly spoke of the teachers as benevolent dictators who insisted on routines such as cleaning the table after snacks and were quick with a genuine hug. Physically, the center shared some aspects of a home activity setting, and some of a child care center. For example, meals were cooked in a kitchen and toddlers were expected to be present and not touch the stove, but there were abundant child-sized toys, furniture, and equipment. As in any child care setting, children competed with age-mates for toys and teacher attention.

Family Day-Care Homes. Our third type of child care activity settings were family day-care homes. In a family day-care home, a person, almost always a woman, takes care of children in her own home. In California, where we conducted our study, family day-care homes must be licensed.

However, in many family day-care homes, including many used by families in our study, the providers do not know that they are required to be licensed or decide not to become licensed.

Caregiving in family day-care homes is usually based on the values of being a "good mother" and loving children (Howes and Sakai, in press). Teacher or providers in family day-care homes are not required to have any particular training in child development. In general, the family day-care providers in our study were distrustful of professional child care teachers and centers, believing that children belonged at home or in homelike environments. The unlicensed family day-care providers in our sample considered themselves to be babysitters or to be doing a favor for a friend rather than providing child care. Therefore, the adults in family day-care home activity settings often have belief systems regarding child care that are similar to those of adults in home activity settings. The major differences are that family day-care adults are caring for children with whom they have no preexisting emotional bonds and that they are caring for more children than are typically attended by most mothers. As a result, the template of motherlike care does not always match the reality.

The activity setting of a family day-care home resembles a home activity setting in that the personnel are limited and predictable. In our sample, family day-care providers worked alone. If other family members were present in the home, child care was not their responsibility. From the child's point of view, this meant that caregiving was predictably received from one person.

Family day-care activity settings also physically resemble home activity settings. The environment is designed for adults and family living. Children in this setting must learn which objects and activities (running down the hall, bouncing on the bed) are prohibited.

Part-Time Unlicensed Care. The families that used unlicensed family day-care in our sample tended to use it for relatively small amounts of time each week. Families used this care less than ten hours a week, primarily as a respite for the nonworking mother. For these children, child care was a regular but infrequent and low-intensity occurrence.

We observed that from the point of view of the family day-care providers these children who came to care relatively infrequently and for short time periods could be relatively easily absorbed into the daily family life of the family day-care home. From the child's point-of-view this meant that caregiving experiences were embedded within housekeeping, trips to the mall, and other informal activities. Therefore, the scripts for caregiving in this activity setting involved fewer routines and rituals than those associated with center care. For example, in this type of family day-care setting, there was no need for snack routines such as stopping playing, cleaning up, washing hands in a group, sitting quietly in small chairs until served a snack, eating together, and putting trash in the wastebasket.

Formal Licensed Care. Two other groups of families used family day-care homes, either part time or full time. These family day-care homes were licensed and had more formal structures and scripts for caregiving. Thus, from the child's point of view, in these family day-care homes, as in the child care centers, daily activities were more predictable than in the informal, unlicensed family day-care homes. Children arrived, engaged in some activities, had snacks, played some more, had lunch, took a nap, went outside to play, and so on. In these more formal family day-care homes and in centers, children were treated as a group. The day was planned for the group of children. In contrast, to a larger extent, in home and informal activity settings, the daily routines were driven by the tasks of home management and by adult preferences.

Although the respective activity settings for caregiving found within homes, family day-care homes, and centers in our samples varied systematically in personnel, beliefs about appropriate care, motives for providing care, and tasks of care, these settings did not vary systematically in sensitivity to children. Within each child care arrangement, caregivers were quite heterogeneous in their responses to children's caregiving needs (Howes and Galluzzo, in press). Likewise, teachers varied greatly in their emotional attachments to children (Sakai and Howes, 1991).

Methods

This study was designed to reflect the range of settings in which toddler-age children receive out-of-home care, and data collection took place within these settings.

Subjects. One hundred and one toddler-age children (mean age at observation = 23.4 months; SD = 3.2), their mothers, and child care teachers participated in this study. The children were drawn from two larger longitudinal studies. Children in sample 1 (N = 67) were enrolled in full-time center-based child care, and children in sample 2 were enrolled in family day-care homes.

Child Care Settings. The five child care settings varied in number of adults present, number of children present, the ratio of children to adults, and the mean length of time that the children attended per day and per week. This descriptive material is presented in Table 2.1. Only in the model child care center group did adult-child ratios approach the standards suggested by experts as appropriate for child care for infants and toddlers. The length of time in child care is consistent with our narrative descriptions of these activity settings.

Procedures. We assessed attachment to mother six months prior to

Table 2.1. Family and Child Care Settings

| | Center (Sample 1) | | Family Day-Care Home (Sample 2) | | |
| | | | Unlicensed | Licensed | |
Sample Features	Model (N = 54)	In Home (N = 13)	Less than Ten Hours/Week (N = 9)	Ten to Twenty Hours/Week (N = 12)	Full Time Licensed (N = 13)
Family Characteristics					
Ethnicity					
European American	36	10	8	12	12
African American	9	1	0	0	0
Asian American	5	2	1	0	1
Latino	4	0	0	0	0
Organization					
Stable	30	7	9	6	11
Stressed	8	6	2	6	2
Disorganized	16	0	0	0	0
Age entered care (in months)	4.2	5.3	11.1	13.6	9.7
N adults	2.3	2	1	1	1
N children	7.4	9.6	4	4.5	5.7
Ratio	3.2	4.8	4	4.5	5.7
Days/Week	4.9	5	1.4	3.1	4.8
Hours/Day	8	8	3.1	5.7	9.3

our assessments of attachment to teacher. Maternal attachment was assessed differently in sample 1 and sample 2. Teacher attachment assessment procedures were identical in both samples. In addition to the attachment assessments, the observers made qualitative descriptive notes during each child care visit. These observations and recurrent discussions within the research team formed the basis for the activity setting descriptions. Each family participating in the study was contacted at three- to six-month intervals in order to facilitate the longitudinal study and to keep us informed of ongoing family events. The same research assistant generally kept in contact with each family and became, in many cases, a confidant and source of support. Not all of the children in the model child care centers received subsidized care. The teachers and our research assistants were blind to the identity of these children. Our ratings of families as stable, stressed, or disorganized were based on the subject coordinators' contacts with the families and child care center director reports of subsidies.

Attachment to Mother. Children's attachment to their mothers was assessed differently across the two samples.

Sample 1. We used the Waters and Deane (1985) Attachment Q-Set to assess the children's relationships with their mothers. The original Attachment Q-Set contains seventy-five items or descriptive statements of the child's behavior toward the adult. These items are sorted into nine piles to form a normal distribution of descriptive statements, ranging from most characteristic (9) to least characteristic (1). The validity of the Attachment Q-Set has been established with the Ainsworth Strange Situation instrument (Vaughn and Waters, 1990).

To complete the Q-Set, two observers each observed at least two arrivals and reunions as the child was dropped off and picked up at child care. There were large variations among mothers, and also for the same mother on different days, in the lengths of arrivals and reunions. At the extremes, the longest observation of an arrival or reunion lasted forty-five minutes, and the shortest lasted less than one minute. Observers completed written descriptions of the children during each observed arrival and reunion and did not complete the Q-Set until they felt confident that they had seen sufficient numbers of subjects to reliably complete the sort. The median number of observed arrivals was five (range two to ten). The median number of observed reunions was also five (range two to eleven). This procedure was validated with Strange Situation classifications (Howes and Hamilton, 1992).

Interobserver reliability was computed on thirty children. Children used for reliability were seen simultaneously by observers prior to the data collection period. Kappa scores on each Q-Set item were computed for interobserver reliability. They ranged from .86 to .94 (median = .93). When two observers saw the same child at different times, there was somewhat lower agreement between observers. The median kappa score was .83 (range .56 to .97).

Sample 2. At twelve months, a standard Ainsworth Strange Situation procedure using children and their mothers in sample 2 was completed under the guidelines presented by Ainsworth, Blehar, Waters, and Wall (1978). The assessments were videotaped, and the behaviors of the infants were coded by Carol Rodning, Brian Vaughn, and Mary Main.

Attachment to Teacher. The Attachment Q-Set was used to assess attachment to primary teacher in both samples. In order to complete the Q-Set, two observers each spent at least two hours on two separate occasions observing each child with the caregiver. We determined the identity of the child's primary caregiver through preliminary observations and discussions with the center directors. To obtain children's security scores, the scores from the two observers' Q-Sets were averaged and then correlated with criterion scores provided by Waters and Deane (1985). The correlation coefficients are the children's security scores. A higher score indicates greater security.

Interobserver reliability was computed on sixty children not in the immediate study. Children used for reliability were seen simultaneously by observers prior to each data collection period. Kappa scores on each Q-Set item were computed for interobserver reliability. They ranged from .83 to .95 (median = .92). When two observers saw the same study child at different times, there was somewhat lower agreement between observers. The median kappa score was .85 (range .45 to .98).

Classification of Q-Sort Data. Children were classified into attachment clusters based on a cluster analysis of a large sample of mother and teacher data collected in an identical manner to this study (Howes and Hamilton, 1992). The cluster analysis yielded clusters for all children conceptually similar to Strange Situation classifications. We used most- and least-characteristic item descriptors of these clusters to categorize children based on their Q-Sort item profiles. Each child's pattern of scores on the Q-Set items was examined. If the child's item score for each of the discriminating items of a cluster was either very high (7,8,9) or very low (1,2,3), depending on the direction of the item, the child was classified into that cluster. Each child fit into only one cluster.

Classification of Attachment Concordance. Children were considered to have concordant maternal and teacher attachment relationships if both relationships were classified as secure, both were classified as avoidant, or both were classified as ambivalent. Children were considered to have nonconcordant maternal and teacher attachments if each relationship received a different attachment classification.

Results

The results are consistent with the hypothesis that children form relationships with their teachers that are similar to their relationships with their mothers, and that differences in the home and child care contexts affect concordance.

Attachment to Mother. Overall, 73 percent of the children were securely attached to their mothers. Maternal attachment classifications varied by assessment procedure and child care activity setting. As assessed with the Q-Sort, children were most likely to be securely attached if they were enrolled in center as opposed to family day care and if their families were stable. Because type of day care and assessment procedure were confounded, we did not make statistical comparisons. Within child care center settings, children were more likely to be classified as secure with their mothers if the Q-Set was used and if they were enrolled in the in-home child care center. These children in the in-home child care centers were also more likely to come from stable families. Fewer of the children from disorganized families were securely attached to their mothers. There were no differences in Strange Situation maternal attachment security based on different amounts of family day care.

Attachment to Teacher. Fifty-nine percent of the children were securely attached to their teachers. Children varied greatly across child care settings in their security of attachment to teacher ($c^2(10) = 56.95$; $p < .001$). Children were most likely to be classified as secure with teachers in the in-home center and full-time family day-care settings. They were least likely to be classified as secure with teachers when they spent ten to twenty hours per week in family day care. Children in less than ten hours of family day care and in model center care were intermediate in percentages of teacher security classifications. Children from disorganized families in model center care were less likely than children from stable or stressed families to form secure relationships with teachers ($c^2(2) = 8.59$, $p \leq .05$).

Concordance of Maternal and Teacher Attachment Classifications Within Each Child Care Setting. The distribution of concordance of maternal and teacher attachment relationships within each child care setting is presented in Table 2.2. Where teacher and mother relationships were concordant, both types were most likely to be secure relationships as opposed to both avoidant or both ambivalent. Because security to mother was not similarly distributed across samples, we analyzed associations between concordance and setting separately by sample. For children in child care centers, mother and teacher attachment relationships were less concordant in the model child care center than in the in-home child care center ($c^2(2) = 7.49$, $p \leq .02$). For children in family day-care homes, mother and teacher attachment relationships were more concordant when children were in family day care less than ten hours a week than when they spent more time in family day care ($c^2(4) = 11.10$, $p \leq .05$).

Concordance of Maternal and Teacher Attachments, Child Care Settings, and Family Type. In order to examine the role of family orga-

Table 2.2. Percentage Distributions of Attachment Relationships and Their Concordance by Child Care Settings and Family Type

| | Center | | | | | Family Day-Care Home | | | | | |
| | Model | | | In Home | | Less than Ten Hours/Week | | Ten to Twenty Hours/Week | | Full Time | |
Family Type	Stable	Stressed	Disorganized	Stable	Stressed	Stable	Stressed	Stable	Stressed	Stable	Stressed
Mother											
Secure	83	100	50	100	86	57	100	75	80	70	64
Avoidant	7	0	13	0	0	43	0	25	20	30	9
Ambivalent	10	0	37	0	14	0	0	0	0	0	27
Teacher											
Secure	60	63	46	100	86	63	100	50	16	100	82
Avoidant	13	13	25	0	0	19	0	67	16	0	9
Ambivalent	27	24	29	0	14	18	0	33	66	0	9
Mother and Teacher Concordant											
Secure	65	63	31	100	71	89	100	33	40	50	45
Avoidant	0	0	0	0	0	0	0	0	0	0	0
Ambivalent	0	0	19	0	0	0	0	0	0	0	0
Nonconcordant	35	37	50	0	29	11	0	67	60	50	55

nization in the concordance of attachment relationships, we calculated concordance separately by family organization within each child care setting (see Table 2.2). Stable and stressed families had the same pattern of concordance and nonconcordance. Within model child care centers, disorganized families were more likely to have concordant ambivalent and nonconcordant relationships, and less likely to have concordant secure relationships, than were stable and stressed families ($c^2(3) = 8.69$, $p \leq .01$).

Discussion

Contextual Constraints on Concordance. Several important findings emerged from our analysis of contextual constraints on maternal and teacher attachment concordance. The children who experienced the most predictable care both at home and in child care appeared more secure with teachers. Children from stable families, enrolled full-time in child care arrangements characterized by regular routines, were most likely to be secure with their teachers. Children who came from disorganized families appear to have challenged even the trained and supported teachers in the model child care centers who introduced regular routines to the children. This was the only context in which children developed concordant ambivalent attachments with teachers and mothers. It was also a context with substantial numbers of nonconcordant, compensatory attachments (insecure with mother and secure with teacher). These compensatory relationships may be a means for these children to master skills that enhance school success.

In general, our findings supported our expectation that degree of overlap between activity settings predicts concordance in maternal and teacher attachments. Three types of child care settings were associated with high concordance. One of these settings directly supports our hypothesis. Children whose child care experience was most like a home activity setting, that is, fewer than ten hours a week in informal, unlicensed, family day care, had high proportions of concordant attachment relationships, both secure and avoidant. We suspect that for these children, who spent relatively little time in child care, the mother-child relationship is much more powerful than the teacher-child relationship.

There was also high concordance for maternal and teacher attachments in the in-home child care center. All of the concordance in this subsample was accounted for by secure relationships. The subsample had an unusually high percentage of secure maternal attachments and a child care setting that appeared to promote secure attachment. Given the overwhelming proportion of secure children, it was mathematically difficult to produce nonconcordance.

The highest levels of nonconcordance between maternal and teacher attachment were found in child care settings that clearly differed from homes in values and goals and in the scripts and routines for caregiving. These settings were the child care centers and the formal, licensed, family day-care homes. In the child care centers, the teachers were clear that they were not mothers and that they were providing a service to families. The child's experience of caregiving, although individualized and appropriate, was different from the caregiving experience at home. The family day-care providers were less clear than the center teachers in distinguishing their values and goals from those of mothers. However, the realities of their caregiving context—large groups of children who remained in their homes for as many as eleven hours a day—required them to treat the children as a group and to find routines for providing care. These constraints appeared more functional for the children who came full time than for the children who came part time. The provider may have found it easier to identify and adapt to the individual needs of a child in her care an average of forty-five hours a week than to constantly readjust her routines for a child who came part time. The child in part-time care may have had a hierarchical system of relationships, whereas the child in full-time care may have had a compensatory, supplementary system of relationships.

Does Context Tell the Entire Story? An underlying and important question for research on children's relationships with their child care teachers is whether these relationships are attachment relationships or merely social relationships heavily influenced by the maternal attachment relationship. Our findings can provide only a partial answer to this question, particularly since the maternal and teacher attachments were not independent in time. They do suggest that children in regular, recurring, and predictable child care arrangements form relationships with their caregiving teachers that are distinct in quality from their maternal attachments. We know from other research that children are most likely to form secure attachment relationships with teachers who provide sensitive care (Howes and Hamilton, 1992), and that when there are several children under the care of one child care teacher, the children form relationships with her that differ in quality (Goossens and Van IJzendoorn, 1990; Sakai and Howes, 1991).

Further research in the area of concordance between teacher and maternal attachment relationships must more closely investigate the role of methodology in the assessment process. We are more satisfied with our assessments of teacher attachment security than with our assessments of maternal attachment security. The Attachment Q-Set was sufficiently flexible for use in a variety of child care settings. We have recently used the revised ninety-item Q-Set and found it to be reliable and valid as well.

Our arrival and departure assessments of maternal attachment were surprisingly similar to Strange Situation assessments, and Q-Sort items distinguishing between children categorized as secure or insecure in the Strange Situation were similar to the discriminatory items found by Vaughn and Waters (1990) using home observations of mothers (Howes and Hamilton, 1992). However, by assessing the mother-child relationship within the child care setting, we risked having teacher behavior influence the maternal-child interaction. We suggest that future research on mother and teacher attachment concordance include home-based observations. This would also allow for a more thorough comparison of home versus child care activity settings. The use of the activity setting model holds promise for increasing our understanding of the important differences among children's caregiving relationships and how each relationship affects an individual child's development.

References

Ainsworth, M.D.S., Blehar, M. C., Waters, E., and Wall, S. *Patterns of Attachment: A Psychological Study of the Strange Situation.* Hillsdale, N.J.: Erlbaum, 1978.

Ainsworth, M.D.S., Bell, S. M., and Stayton, D. J. "Infant-Mother Attachment and Social Development: Socialization as a Product of Reciprocal Responses to Signals." In M. P. Richards (ed.), *The Integration of the Child into the Social World.* Cambridge, England: Cambridge University Press, 1974.

Bowlby, J. *Attachment and Loss.* Vol. 1: *Attachment.* (Rev. ed.) New York: Basic Books, 1982.

Bretherton, I. "Attachment Theory: Retrospective and Prospect." In I. Bretherton and E. Waters (eds.), *Growing Points of Attachment: Theory and Research.* Monographs of the Society for Research in Child Development, vol. 50, nos. 1–2 (serial no. 209). Chicago: University of Chicago Press, 1985.

Bridges, L. J., Connell, J. P., and Belsky, J. "Similarities in Infant-Mother and Infant-Father Interaction in the Strange Situation." *Developmental Psychology,* 1988, 24, 92–100.

Eheart, B. K., and Leavitt, R. L. "Family Day Care Discrepancies Between Intended and Observed Caregiving Practices." *Early Childhood Research Quarterly,* 1989, 4, 145–162.

Goossens, F. A., and Van IJzendoorn, M. H. "Quality of Infants' Attachment to Professional Caregivers: Relation to Infant-Parent Attachment and Daycare Characteristics." *Child Development,* 1990, 61, 832–837.

Howes, C., and Galluzzo, D. "Adult Socialization of Children's Play in Child Care." In H. Goelman (ed.), *Child Care and Play.* Albany: State University of New York Press, in press.

Howes, C., and Sakai, L. M. "Family Day Care for Infants and Toddlers." In D. Peters and A. Pence (eds.), *Family Day Care: Current Research for Informed Public Policy.* New York: Teachers College Press, in press.

Howes, C., and Hamilton, C. E. "Children's Relationships with Child Care Teachers: Stability and Concordance with Parental Attachments." *Child Development,* 1992, 63, 867–878.

Matheson, C. C., Rose, A., and Howes, C. "Internal Working Models and Multiple Attachments." Unpublished manuscript, University of California, Los Angeles, 1991.

Sakai, L. M., and Howes, C. "Quality of Attachment: (Dis)Similarity Between Two Children and the Same Caregiver." Unpublished manuscript, University of California, Los Angeles, 1991.

Schaffer, H. R., and Emerson, P. E. *The Development of Social Attachments in Infancy.* Monographs of the Society for Research in Child Development, vol. 29, no. 3 (serial no. 94). Chicago: University of Chicago Press, 1964.

Sroufe, L. A. "The Role of Infant-Caregiver Attachment in Development." In J. Belsky and T. Nezworski (eds.), *Clinical Implications of Attachment.* Hillsdale, N.J.: Erlbaum, 1988.

Sroufe, L. A., and Fleeson, J. "The Coherence of Family Relationships." In R. A. Hinde and J. Stevenson-Hinde (eds.), *Relationships Within Families: Mutual Influences.* Oxford, England: Clarendon Press, 1988.

Vaughn, B. E., and Waters, E. "Attachment Behavior at Home and in the Laboratory: Q-Sort Observations and Strange Situation Classifications of One-Year-Olds." *Child Development,* 1990, *61,* 1965–1973.

Waters, E., and Deanne, K. E. "Defining and Assessing Individual Differences in Attachment Relationships: Q-Methodology and the Organization of Behavior in Infancy and Early Childhood." In I. Bretherton and E. Waters (eds.), *Growing Points of Attachment: Theory and Research.* Monographs of the Society for Research in Child Development, vol. 50, nos. 1–2 (serial no. 209). Chicago: University of Chicago Press, 1985.

Weisner, T. S. "A Cross-Cultural Perspective: Ecocultural Niches of Middle Childhood." In A. Collins (ed.), *The Elementary School Years: Understanding Development During Middle Childhood.* Washington, D.C.: National Academy Press, 1984.

Weisner, T. S. "An Ecological and Activity Setting Model of Socialization." Unpublished manuscript, University of California, Los Angeles, 1988.

Weisner, T. S., and Wilson-Mitchell, J. E. "Nonconventional Family Life-Styles and Sex Typing in Six-Year-Olds." *Child Development,* 1990, *61,* 1915–1933.

CAROLLEE HOWES is professor, Graduate School of Education, University of California, Los Angeles. Her research interests include development of social relationships and social communication with adults and peers.

CATHERINE C. MATHESON is research associate, Department of Psychiatry, University of California, Los Angeles. Her research interests include culture and development and children's relationships with multiple attachment figures.

Teacher-child and parent-child relationships show behavioral similarities and differences related to context and relationship quality.

A Comparison of Young Children's Relationships with Mothers and Teachers

Claire E. Hamilton, Carollee Howes

Child care is becoming a part of the lives of increasing numbers of young children, both infants and preschoolers. Children enrolled in child care do form relationships with their teachers and they do maintain relationships with their parents. Although these relationships may serve similar functions, especially in infancy, differences exist in the nature of the social interaction that takes place between children and their parents and between children and their teachers. In this chapter, we compare the social interaction that occurs between children and their mothers and between children and their teachers on two levels. Our first focus is on the specific behaviors that might differentiate relationships with teachers and mothers. Our second focus, drawing on attachment theory, concerns differences in the quality of teacher and mother relationships.

Children's Relationships with Teachers and Mothers

Many of the routines that, in an attachment theory framework, are associated with the development of attachment relationships are man-

Some of the teacher-child and mother-child attachment Q-Sets were gathered as part of the doctoral dissertation of Darlene Galluzzo, the master's theses of Virginia Davila and Ellen Wolpow, and the National Child Care Staffing Study. Thank you for making the data available to us. Thanks also to the research team who worked on our study: Kristen Droege, Darlene Galluzzo, Annette Groen, Catherine Matheson, Lisabeth Meyers, Jacquline Moore, Leslie Phillipsen, Ellen Wolpow, and Fang Wu. The research could not have been conducted without the cooperation of the participating families and child care teachers.

aged by both parents and teachers. Attachment theory (Bowlby, 1982) suggests that children develop attachment relationships through ongoing interactions with caregiving adults. Both teachers and parents engage in caregiving interactions, and children are dependent on their teachers as well as their parents. Teachers settle children down for naps, they give kisses and hugs to children upset from bumps and scrapes, they help children handle the stress of daily separations from their parents, they manage diapering and toileting routines, and, on a basic level, they ensure that children are kept physically safe. Many of the caregiving interactions that are associated with the development of attachment relationships are managed by both teachers and parents. Despite the similarity of the activities that occur between children and their teachers and parents, there are certainly differences in the contexts of these activities. How do these contextual differences influence children's social behavior with different partners?

Children's behaviors with mothers and teachers may differ because of the contexts in which these interactions take place, home versus child care center, and because of the different roles that teachers and parents play in children's lives. Howes and Matheson (this volume) have adopted an activity setting perspective in contrasting the contexts of home and child care. Care for children in the home is usually the role of one or two related adults, is often accompanied by other household tasks, and is not generally associated with the presence of age-mates. In contrast, children in child care are cared for by nonrelated adults, often several of them, in larger groups of age-mates, in a setting where the primary goal is child care. Children's behaviors with teachers and parents may vary because of these differences in context. In our study, children were observed with both mothers and teachers in their child care setting. The physical setting did not vary; however, the roles and scripts for behavior did vary. Children's behaviors with mothers were observed as they were dropped off and picked up at child care, whereas their behaviors with teachers were observed over the course of the day. For teachers, the major emphasis was on the care and management of a group of children, not one particular child. For mothers, the focus was on settling their child into the child care setting and getting themselves off to work, or on reestablishing their relationship with their own child at the end of the day. For children, there may also have been different expectations or scripts for behavior. During reunions and separations, they too had to sever or reestablish relationships with their mothers. In contrast, during our observations of them with their teachers, separations were less likely to occur and a greater variety of social partners were available, including peers.

Teachers and parents also differ in the roles that they play in children's lives. The major difference is in the permanence and constancy of these adults. Parents are, in the ideal world, consistent partners in their children's lives; teachers are not. High rates of teacher turnover in excess of 40 percent per year (Whitebrook, Howes, and Phillips, 1990), center policies and state regulations mandating age-segregated classrooms, and changes in child care arrangements initiated by parents mean that most children will be expected to form relationships with several different teachers over the course of early childhood. Additionally, children enrolled in child care centers are usually cared for by more than one adult over the course of a day. In short, teachers are not a permanent part of children's lives.

Mothers and teachers may also differ in how they perceive their respective roles. Teachers, especially with older preschoolers, may engage in fewer caregiving interactions and may define their role as instructional rather than caregiving. Although mothers certainly informally instruct their children, they are probably less likely to assume an instructional over a caregiving role. These differences in roles may also influence children's social behaviors.

Children's Social Behaviors Within Mother and Teacher Relationships

The second focus of this chapter draws on attachment theory in exploring children's social behaviors within their relationships with mothers and teachers. As noted earlier, attachment theory (Bowlby, 1982) suggests that children develop attachment relationships through ongoing interactions with caregiving adults. There is clear empirical and theoretical support that children form attachment relationships with their mothers. It is less clear if children form attachment relationships with their teachers.

We earlier discussed similarities in the caregiving interactions of teachers and parents. Both parents and teachers are responsible for providing physical and emotional support for children in their care. In our study, however, we proposed that teachers and mothers might differ not only in their permanence but also in their perceptions of themselves as caregivers. If attachment relationships are derived from recurring caregiving interactions, then children may not form attachment relationships with their teachers because teachers are less consistent partners and because teachers may not view themselves as caregivers, particularly of preschool-age children. Two bodies of research bear on the issue of whether children do indeed form attachment relationships with their teachers. The first has focused on whether or not similarities exist between mother-child relationships and teacher-child relationships, and the second has related child outcomes to the quality of teacher-child relationships.

Researchers who have used the Strange Situation (Ainsworth, Blehar,

Waters, and Wall, 1978) to assess the quality of teacher-child relationships have found that the patterns identified in the mother-child relationships (avoidant, secure, and resistant) also exist between children and their teachers (Ainslie and Anderson, 1984) and that the distribution of these patterns is similar (Goossens and Van IJzendoorn, 1990). In our own research, using Waters and Deane's (1985) Attachment Q-Sort, we have also been able to identify similar patterns of attachment relationships (Howes and Hamilton, 1992a). The security of teacher-child relationships, as with mothers, was also related to the amount of teacher responsivity and involvement (Howes and Hamilton, 1992a; Whitebrook, Howes, and Phillips, 1990). Additionally, attachment security with teachers seems unrelated to children's ages (Howes and Hamilton, 1992b), suggesting that teachers do serve as caregiving adults for children throughout early childhood.

Attachment theory also suggests that children, through attachment relationships, form internal working models of self that are used to interpret their experiences (Bretherton, 1987). The child's use of this internal working model is the basis for expecting links between maternal attachment history and later child adaptive competence. Patterns of maternal attachment are related to a variety of social, emotional, and cognitive outcomes (Lamb, Thompson, Gardner, and Charnov, 1985). If children form attachment relationships with their teachers, we would expect to find similar relations between patterns of teacher attachment and child outcomes.

Attachment relationships may have particular relevance to children's ability to form and maintain new relationships. Social competence, the ability to interact successfully with peers, has been studied in reference to both mother and teacher attachments. Preschoolers with secure maternal attachment relationships are more socially competent with their peers than are those with insecure attachment histories (Sroufe, 1983; Waters, Wippman, and Sroufe, 1979). Children with secure attachment relationships with their teachers also seem to be more socially competent (Howes, Rodning, Galluzzo, and Myers, 1988). When the influence of both maternal and nonparental attachment relationships are considered, the attachment relationships with nonparental caregivers, teachers or metaplot, may in fact have a greater influence on the development of children's social competence with peers than do their maternal attachment relationships (Howes and others, 1990; Oppenheim, Sagi, and Lamb, 1988). Social competence with peers is only one outcome that has been considered in relation to the influence of nonparental attachments. Pianta and Nimetz (1991) used a teacher questionnaire designed to reflect teachers' internal working models of their relationships with children. Children's competence in the classroom was associated with teacher relationship ratings.

These empirical findings lend support to our theoretical assumption that children do form attachment relationships with their teachers. There are, however, real differences in teacher-child and mother-child relationships, particularly in the consistency of these relationships. The research base on children's relationships with their mothers is extensive; far less is known about the quality of children's relationships with their teachers. Examination and comparison of how children with different patterns of relationships interact within these relationships with teachers and mothers will add to our understanding of how children form and maintain relationships with teachers. We expect that children's social behaviors discriminate attachment classifications within both mother and teacher relationships. Children who are securely attached should demonstrate greater competence and skill in negotiating social interaction than shown by children with insecure patterns of attachment.

Measurement Issues in Attachment Research

Measurement of the quality of attachment between children and their teachers is a matter of concern. The standard method of assessing maternal attachment, the Strange Situation (Ainsworth, Blehar, Waters, and Wall, 1978), was validated through extensive observations of maternal-child behavior in the home and is applicable only for children between twelve and eighteen months of age. Researchers who have used the Strange Situation to assess the quality of teacher relationships have found that the patterns of attachment observed between children and teachers are similar to those between children and mothers, though there is the suggestion that the Strange Situation procedure may not have captured the qualitative differences within teacher relationships (Ainslie and Anderson, 1984; Goossens and Van IJzendoorn, 1990). The lack of extensive center-based observations that correspond to the home observations done by Ainsworth, Blehar, Waters, and Wall (1978) makes it difficult to determine whether the Strange Situation is an appropriate procedure for assessing nonmaternal attachment relationships.

Waters and Deane (1985) have developed a method of assessing attachment based on naturalistic observations of children's behaviors with their caregivers. While the validity of the Strange Situation rests on home observations, the Waters and Deane Attachment Q-Sort examines attachment relationships through observations. This measure may be more appropriate for assessing nonmaternal attachment. Additionally, it is designed to measure attachment throughout early childhood. We used the Attachment Q-Sort to observe children's interactions with mothers and teachers. This measure has been used previously in child care research (Howes and others, 1990; Whitebrook, Howes, and Phillips, 1990) and contains a variety of descriptive statements about children's interactions with adults.

Many of the Q-Set statements directly tap dimensions of attachment, while others describe more generally the social behaviors occurring between children and their caregivers. We used the wide range of Q-Set items to examine the differences between children's relationships with mothers and teachers. In examining differences within teacher and mother relationships, we focused on the items specifically describing social interactions, rather than on those directly designed to differentiate attachment security. In this study, we were concerned not with how individual children vary in their interactions with teachers and their mothers but rather with the differences and similarities of teacher-child and mother-child relationships. We used two independent samples, one of children with their teachers and another of children with their mothers.

Methods

This research involved a large number of children in varied child care settings and multiple measures of relationships with teachers and parents as well as measures of children's social behavior.

Sample. Four hundred and forty-one children participated in this research. Three hundred thirty-one children (171 males and 160 females) were observed with their teachers, and 110 (45 males and 65 females) were observed with their mothers. The mother and teacher samples were independent. The children ranged in age from ten to fifty-six months (mean age thirty-six months) in both groups and were heterogeneous with respect to ethnicity, socioeconomic status, and family structure. Children were observed in over eighty community child care centers and family day-care homes. The child care settings varied in geographical location and in the socioeconomic status of the families served. The children were all enrolled full time and 80 percent had entered child care prior to their first birthday. All of the children had received care from their primary teacher for at least four months prior to observation. The quality of the child care arrangements was assessed by the Harms and Clifford (1980) Environmental Rating Scale and varied from 1.10 to 6.90 on a 7-point scale ($M = 3.71$). A score of 3 on this measure indicates acceptable quality.

Procedures. The primary assessment procedure used the Waters and Deane (1985) attachment Q-Set and an index of the attachment relationship between child and adult.

Relationships with Teachers. We used the Waters and Deane (1985) Attachment Q-Set to assess the children's relationships with their primary teachers. The Attachment Q-Set contains seventy-five items or descriptive statements of the child's behavior toward the adult. The items are sorted into nine piles to form a normal distribution of most characteristic (9) to least characteristic (1) descriptive statements. Following pilot work in child care arrangements, we eliminated ten items because they were not observed within child care settings. In order to complete the Q-Set, two observers each spent at least two hours on two separate occasions observing the primary teacher. The sorts for both observers were then averaged. We determined the identity of the child's primary teacher by careful preliminary observations to determine which teachers were available to and preferred by the child. We also asked center directors and head teachers to identify primary teachers for each child.

Interobserver reliability was computed on sixty children who did not participate in the study. Children used for reliability were seen simultaneously by observers prior to each data collection period. Kappa scores on each Q-Set item were computed for interobserver reliability (range .83 to .95, median = .92). When two observers saw the same study child at different times, there was somewhat lower agreement between observers (range .45 to .98, median = .85).

Children's relationships with teachers were classified using a cluster analysis procedure conducted on a subset of the Q-Set items (Howes and Hamilton, 1992a). These cluster-derived classifications are similar to those identified in the Ainsworth Strange Situation (Ainsworth, Blehar, Waters, and Wall, 1978) and were externally correlated with observations of teacher sensitivity and involvement (Howes and Hamilton, 1992a). To be classified as secure, a child had to receive a 7 or higher rating on all of the following Q-Set items: predominant mood is happy, easily comforted, solicits comfort, greets adult spontaneously, flexible in communication, and obedient; and a 3 or lower rating on all of the following items: unaware of adult changes in location, no physical contact with adult, expects the adult to be unresponsive, and not compliant. To be rated as avoidant, a child had to receive a 7 or higher rating on all of the following items: unaware of adult changes in location, no physical contact, expects adult to be unresponsive, demanding initiation; and a 3 or lower rating on the item cries often. To be rated as ambivalent, a child had to receive a 7 or higher rating on all of the following items: expects adult to be unresponsive, demanding and impatient, distressed social interactions, demanding interaction, and cries often; and a 3 or lower rating on the item physical contact. Forty-five children (14 percent) had avoidant relationships, 242 children (73 percent) had secure relationships, and 44 (13 percent) had resistant relationships.

Relationships with Mothers. The Attachment Q-Set was used similarly to assess the child's relationship with the mother. Two observers each observed the child at least twice being picked up and dropped off at child care. Observers completed written descriptions of the child during each observed arrival and reunion and did not complete the Q-Set until they felt confident that they had seen sufficient numbers of subjects to reliably complete the sort. The median number of observed arrivals was five (range two to ten). The median number of observed reunions was also five (range two to eleven). Observations of child care separations and reunions have been validated with Strange Situation behaviors (Blanchard and Main, 1979; Ragozin, 1980) and in our previous research (Howes and Hamilton, 1992a). Our cluster-derived classifications were similar to those obtained with the Strange Situation procedure.

Interobserver reliability was computed on thirty children. Children used for reliability were seen simultaneously by observers prior to the data collection period. Kappa scores on each Q-Set item were computed for interobserver reliability (range .86 to .94, median = .93). As with teachers, there was somewhat lower agreement between observers when children were seen at different times (median Kappa = .83, range .56 to .97). Children's relationships with mothers were classified identically to the procedures for teachers. Eleven (9 percent) children were classified as avoidant, eighty-three (76 percent) as secure, and sixteen (14 percent) as resistant.

Analysis Plan. In our analyses, we focused on three questions: (1) What Q-Set items best discriminate children's relationships with teachers and mothers? (2) Using a subset of the Q-Set items, excluding those defining attachment, what items differentiate children with secure, avoidant, or resistant teacher attachment relationships? (3) Using the same subset of items, what items differentiate children with secure, avoidant, or resistant mother attachment relationships? To address the first question, we performed a discriminant function analysis using identity of partner (mother or teacher) as the discriminating variable. To address both the second and third questions, we analyzed the mother and teacher groups separately, using attachment classification (avoidant, secure, or resistant) as the discriminating variable.

Results

The results identify a number of similarities and differences between children's relationships with their mothers and teachers.

Comparing Children's Behaviors with Mothers and Teachers. The Attachment Q-Set items are specifically designed to assess children's attachment relationships with caregiving adults, but the Q-Set includes a broad range of interactive behaviors. In determining which items to include in the analyses, we reduced our sixty-five-item sort to those variables specifically related to the child's interaction with adults. The eliminated items included those not directly related to relationships, for example, "nurturing toys," "presence of tension movements," and "does not share." Table 3.1 presents the means and standard deviations of the forty-one items retained in the analyses for mothers and teachers. The items were conceptually grouped.

Table 3.1. Attachment Q-Sort Items

	Teachers		Mothers	
Items	M	SD	M	SD
Compliance				
Not compliant	3.32	1.62	3.71	1.52
Upset by negative evaluation	4.46	1.32	4.94	1.05
Self-control	4.75	1.03	4.62	1.10
Obedient	6.82	1.58	6.43	1.56
Emotionality				
Does not cry from minor injury	5.99	1.48	5.43	1.09
Frequently starts crying	6.59	2.00	3.97	1.70
Easily angry	4.92	1.75	3.90	1.64
Cries often	3.75	2.22	4.06	2.50
Expressive	7.14	1.58	6.79	1.43
Demanding/Impatient	3.53	1.71	4.17	1.85
Happy	7.19	1.60	6.99	1.96
Avoidance				
Does not enjoy physical play	3.97	1.50	4.35	.91
Does not solicit physical contact	4.54	1.36	3.58	1.47
Does not enjoy physical contact	3.39	1.95	3.08	2.18
Expects unresponsivity	2.34	1.62	3.71	1.51
Comfort				
Easily comforted	6.41	1.31	5.98	1.39
Actively asks for comfort	5.50	1.47	5.14	.77
Easily distracted from distress	6.33	1.35	5.70	1.33
Solicits comfort	6.12	1.70	5.93	1.21
Prefers contact with known adult	4.27	1.97	6.96	1.44
Rarely asks for help	3.92	2.24	3.87	1.33
Accepts assistance	3.82	2.66	6.15	1.52
Social interaction				
Laughs easily with adult	4.04	2.46	5.02	1.57
Affective sharing	6.27	1.87	5.36	1.71
Indirect/Hesitant	3.18	2.05	3.56	1.36
Maximum good mood with adult	5.18	1.88	4.62	1.67
Interacts directly	6.83	1.98	5.74	1.66
Maintains social interaction	6.52	2.14	4.53	1.64
Warm approaches to adult	4.73	1.81	6.55	1.61
Distressed with difficult interaction	4.50	1.46	4.92	1.55
Demanding when initiating	6.68	2.08	4.54	1.72
Approaches adult to interact	7.16	1.64	6.04	1.73
Physical orientation to adult				
Brief bouts away	4.22	1.83	5.06	1.66
Tries to follow adult	4.94	2.17	4.55	1.96
Unaware when adult moves	4.58	2.19	3.29	1.89
Spontaneously checks in	5.21	1.57	6.34	1.50
Distressed when adult moves	4.69	1.90	3.99	1.82
Cries when separated	4.15	1.74	2.89	2.10
Aware of social environment	7.41	1.56	7.10	1.60
Independent	4.79	2.13	6.38	2.54
Proximity/Exploration cycles evident	3.82	1.72	3.31	1.49

Compliance includes items related to the child's obedience to the adult and reaction to negative evaluation. Emotionality refers to the child's overall affective behavior, whether the child is easily angered, frequently cries, or is positive in reference to the caregiver. Avoidance items are those that relate to children's engagement and expectations regarding physical closeness with the adult. Comfort items include those that assess the child's use of the adult for comfort and for assistance. The social interaction variables specifically relate to the children's interactions with the adult, the quality of their moods, their styles of initiation (warm or demanding), and whether they work to maintain the interactions. Finally, the items grouped as physical orientation are those directed toward the child's awareness of the adult's location in the environment and their responses to separation from the adult.

A discriminant function analysis was performed on the forty-one items contained in Table 3.1, using mother versus teacher as the discriminating variable. One discriminant function was calculated with $\chi^2(41) = 472.22$, $p < .001$. Table 3.2 contains the standardized canonical discriminant function coefficients and the descriptive statistics. We drew on the univariate statistics in interpreting the predictor variables for the discriminant function. Mother and teacher means varied significantly ($p < .05$ with Bonferroni correction) on six of the seven predictor variables with standardized canonical discriminant coefficients above .30.

Children were more likely with their mothers than with their teachers to cry upon separation, to engage in bouts of crying, to expect their mothers to be responsive, and to be aware of their mothers' changes in location. Children were more likely to be demanding with their teachers than with their mothers.

Overall, 94 percent of the children were correctly classified into the teacher or mother group. One hundred and five (95 percent) children observed with mothers were predicted to be in the mother group and 6 (5 percent) were incorrectly predicted to be in the teacher group. For teachers, 308 (93 percent) of the children were correctly predicted, while 23 (7 percent) were incorrectly assigned to the mother group. It is important to remember when evaluating these classification results that children were observed with either mothers or teachers; we were not examining differences in individual children's interactions with mothers and teachers.

Comparing Children's Behaviors Within Teacher Relationships. To compare children's social interaction within teacher relationships and across attachment classifications, we reduced the set of items to those that we had identified as specifically characterizing social interaction. We excluded items that were used to assign children to attachment classifications.

To identify items descriptive of social interactions within teacher-

Table 3.2. Mother Versus Teacher Relationships

Items	Standardized Canonical Discriminant Function	$F_{(1,439)}$	Teacher		Mother	
			M	SD	M	SD
Unaware adult moves	.65188	32.51[a]	3.25	.88	4.58	2.19
Frequently cries	.60637	156.10[a]	3.95	1.65	6.59	2.00
Expects no response	-.48884	62.42[a]	3.78	1.52	2.34	1.62
Maximum good mood	.46589	7.39[a]	4.64	1.68	5.18	1.88
Cries when separated	.43781	41.27[a]	2.85	2.10	4.15	1.74
Demanding	.39031	94.07[a]	4.54	1.74	6.68	2.08
Dislikes contact	.38617	1.78	3.09	2.19	3.87	1.95
Asks for comfort	.34770	6.21	5.14	.77	5.50	1.47
Rarely asks for help	.34745	.05	3.85	1.33	3.92	2.24

[a] $p < .05$

child relationships that related to teacher-child attachment status, we again performed a discriminant function analysis. Three hundred and thirty-one observations of children with their teachers were included in the analysis. The discriminating variable was cluster-derived attachment classification (avoidant, resistant, or secure). Two functions (see Table 3.3) were calculated, the first accounting for 72 percent of the variance and the second for 28 percent ($\chi^2[18]$ = 250.94, $p < .001$ and $\chi^2[8]$ = 78.973, $p < .001$, respectively).

The first function contained predictor variables associated with approach style (warm and direct) and the second contained variables associated with affective quality of the interaction (no affective sharing and distressed by difficult social interaction). Table 3.4 contains the differences among the means on predictor variables. These means were compared using Tukey's honestly significant difference.

Children classified as secure with teacher engaged in the most affective sharing during interactions, were the least hesitant, and were the most likely to maintain the interaction. Children with avoidant relationships were the most hesitant to interact. Those children with resistant classifications were least likely to be indirect and more likely than secure or avoidant children to approach warmly and be distressed when the social interaction was difficult.

Overall, 98 percent of the children were correctly classified. One hundred percent were correctly classified as avoidant ($N = 45$), 98 percent as secure ($N = 238$), and 96 percent as resistant ($N = 42$). Table 3.5 contains the actual and predicted classifications. The greatest error in predicted group membership was 5 percent and accounted for children who were actually secure being incorrectly classified as resistant.

Table 3.3. Discriminant Functions with Teacher and Mother Relationships

| | Standardized Discriminant Function Coefficients | | | |
| | Function 1 | | Function 2 | |
Items	Teachers	Mothers	Teachers	Mothers
Indirect/Hesitant	-.4204	.1697	-.2351	-.4153
Approaches adult to interact	.2496	.0180	.0945	.0960
Maintains social interaction	.3461	.3515	-.0994	.0746
Interacts directly	.2507	.0861	.2350	.7252
Maximum good mood	.1653	.1985	.2048	.5339
Affective sharing	.2465	-.1329	-.6118	.6605
Distressed difficult interaction	-.0851	-.4045	.6058	.1098
Warm approach	.5460	.6326	.3886	-.3420
Laughs easily	.0698	.5041	.1154	.1269

Table 3.4. Discriminating Behaviors in Teacher and Mother Relationships

Items	F	Avoidant M	SD	Secure M	SD	Resistant M	SD
Indirect/Hesitant							
Teacher	64.44^a	5.80_x	1.85	2.66_y	1.67	3.99_z	2.08
Mother	2.55	4.18	2.14	3.58	1.23	3.00	1.32
Approaches adult to interact							
Teacher	39.72^a	5.51_x	1.83	7.56_y	1.34	6.64_z	1.74
Mother	4.13^a	6.45_x	1.78	6.20_x	1.55	4.94_y	2.24
Maintains social interaction							
Teacher	42.58^a	4.62_x	1.80	7.09_y	1.88	5.27_x	2.15
Mother	4.14^a	4.05	1.97	4.77_x	1.47	3.59_y	2.02
Interacts directly							
Teacher	37.20^a	5.04_x	1.77	7.33_y	1.79	5.93_x	1.81
Mother	6.46	4.50_x	1.64	6.02_y	1.56	5.00	1.66
Maximum good mood							
Teacher	30.35^a	3.33_x	1.87	5.43_y	1.65	5.73_y	2.02
Mother	2.87	3.64	1.42	4.82	1.64	4.28	1.97
Affective sharing							
Teacher	41.07^a	3.53_x	1.93	6.76_y	1.56	4.55_x	2.02
Mother	2.49	4.41	1.41	5.38	1.68	5.88	1.92
Distressed difficult interaction							
Teacher	27.18^a	4.84_x	1.54	4.26_y	1.77	5.52_x	2.14
Mother	19.08^a	5.50	1.70	4.51_x	1.32	6.72_y	1.25
Warm approach							
Teacher	10.50^a	4.33_x	1.68	4.60_x	1.77	5.84_y	1.82
Mother	30.22^a	5.58_x	.87	7.06_y	1.23	4.38_x	1.83
Laughs easily							
Teacher	5.55	3.33	2.58	3.99	2.36	5.02	2.64
Mother	7.98^a	4.05_x	1.13	5.33_y	1.54	4.00_x	1.38

Note: Means not sharing subscripts are significantly different. $F(2,238)$ for teachers and $F(2,108)$ for mothers.
[a] $p < .05$

Comparing Children's Behavior Within Mother-Child Relationships. The same variables and same method were used to identify Q-Set items within mother-child relationships that were related to mother-child attachment status. Two discriminant functions were calculated. The first function had $\chi^2(18) = 101.53$, $p < .001$, accounting for 85 percent of the variance, and the second $\chi^2(8) = 19.57$, $p < .01$, accounting for 15 percent of the variance. Table 3.3 contains the standardized canonical discriminant function coefficients for each of the functions. Variables loading on the first function included laughing easily around the adult, warm approaches, and a lack of distress at difficult social interactions. Those loading on the second function were affective sharing, a lack of hesitancy in interacting, a maximum good mood with the adult, and a direct style of interaction. All of the children were correctly classified using these two discriminant functions.

Differences in group means were again used to interpret the functions, using Tukey's honestly significant difference for the predictor variables (see Table 3.4). Children with secure maternal attachment relationships were more likely to laugh around the adult, most likely to warmly approach the adult for interaction, and more likely than those with resistant, but not avoidant, attachment classifications to maintain the interaction and not to be distressed by difficult social interactions.

Comparing Mother and Teacher Attachment Relationships. The pattern of variables associated with the two functions were not similar for mothers and teachers. For teachers, the affective quality of the interaction was associated with the second function, and the child's style of approach clearly characterized the first function. Figure 3.1 contains a scatterplot of the group centroids for mother and teacher attachment classifications.

In teacher-child relationships, the first function clearly discriminated those children with secure or resistant classifications from those with avoidant classifications. The second function then isolated the avoidant and resistant classifications. In the mother-child relationships,

Table 3.5. Actual and Predicted
Group Membership Within Teacher Relationships

Actual Group	N	Predicted Group		
		Avoidant	Secure	Resistant
Avoidant	45	45	0	0
Secure	242	2 (1%)	238 (98%)	2 (1%)
Resistant	44	0	2 (5%)	42 (96%)

Note: Overall correct classification is 98 percent.

Figure 3.1. Group Centroids Within
Mother and Teacher Relationships

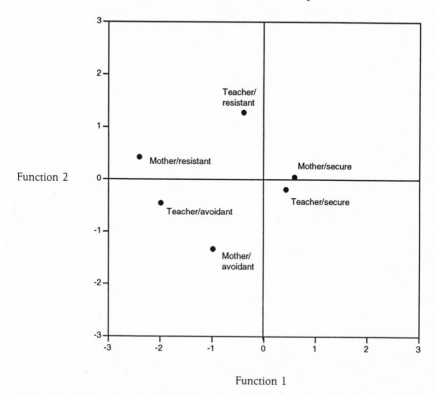

Function 1

there was a less clear loading of affective and approach behaviors on the two functions, and children with secure or avoidant classifications were more similar on the first function, unlike children with resistant classifications. Despite the differences in the patterning of the variables discriminating mother and teacher attachment relationships, children's social behaviors did distinguish between these relationships.

Discussion

We first asked if children differed in the behaviors that they directed toward mothers and teachers. Our results indicate that behaviors did clearly discriminate between relationships. In particular, children's moods, expectations of adult responsiveness, awareness of adult location, and reliance on adult for comfort and assistance differed between and within relationships. Some of these differences in the behaviors that children direct toward teachers and mothers may be linked to the context in which these interactions occur. In this study, examination of contextual differences was limited. Children's relationships with both mothers and teachers were assessed in the child care setting. Children and their mothers were observed during separations and reunions. Although the behaviors that children direct toward their mothers during these reunions and separations may be similar to the behaviors that they direct toward mothers in the Strange Situation (Blanchard and Main, 1979; Ragozin, 1980), these behaviors may not capture the full range of behaviors directed toward their mothers in other settings. Additionally, reunions and separations are likely to be stressful times for children even if they are everyday occurrences. Behaviors such as crying when separated, frequent crying, and awareness of the adults' locations may be more salient in reunion and separation episodes.

There are suggestions, however, that the broader contextual differences between home and child care settings are implicated. Children are more demanding when initiating to teachers. In the child care setting, children may need to be more forceful in their bids for attention because teachers are often engaged with other children and adults. For the same reasons, children may also perceive teachers as being less available than mothers. Mothers in home and in our observed reunions and separations are likely to be caring for one or perhaps two children; children may expect mothers to be more responsive. We should, however, be careful in interpreting this finding. Children do not expect their teachers to be unresponsive. The difference between the group means indicates both adults to be responsive; the difference is relative.

We focused second on the extent to which the quality of children's relationships with either mothers or teachers is related to their social behaviors with that adult. Children's social behaviors discriminated avoidant, secure, and resistant relationships with both mothers and teachers. With both mothers and teachers, children's affective sharing, warm approach to the adult, hesitancy to interact, distress at difficult social interaction, and ability to maintain the social interaction discriminated between attachment classifications. For mothers, but not teachers, children's directness and positive mood also contributed to the discrimination.

Children with secure attachment relationships approached teachers directly, maintained their social interaction, and seemed to enjoy the interactions. They were more socially adept at achieving and maintaining social interaction with their teachers. With mothers, though the behaviors differed, secure children seemed to adapt to the setting in a competent manner. Even during reunions and separations, they were more warm in their approaches to their mothers and, despite the stress that might be associated with these events, maintained positive affect in their interactions. One striking difference did emerge. Children with resistant teacher relationships were the most likely to warmly approach the teachers, whereas, for mother relationships, children with secure relationships were most likely to have a warm approach. Sroufe (1983) found that children with resistant maternal attachment histories were more dependent on their preschool teachers. Children with resistant teacher relationships may also be more dependent and may exhibit more warm approaches relative to their securely attached peers. For mothers, the association between security and warm approaches is consistent with Strange Situation behavior (Ainsworth, Blehar, Waters, and Wall, 1978) and reflects the context of the observations.

Sroufe (1983; Sroufe and Waters, 1977) has conceptualized the development of a secure maternal attachment relationship in infancy as a measure of adaptive competence. It would be expected from this perspective that, in later developmental periods and in related contexts, children with secure attachment relationships will exhibit more competent behaviors than will their insecurely attached peers. Research on the correlates of maternal attachment relationships lends support to this perspective (Lamb, Thompson, Gardner, and Charnov, 1985). Our examination of the behaviors discriminating among attachment classifications within mother and teacher relationships supports this notion that secure attachment is related to adaptive competence. The differences between the behaviors that discriminated attachment classifications within mother and teacher relationships are related to the different social settings that the children were negotiating. For mothers, this setting included daily separations and reunions with one social partner; for teachers, the setting included the broad range of activities occurring throughout the day. The demands for children in these settings are quite different. In one instance, children are handling the transition between home and child care, and either the departure of a primary attachment figure or a reunion with that same partner at the end of a long day. In the other instance, children are engaging in social interaction across a wide range of activities in competition for attention with other children and with other adults. We would not expect that behaviors indicative of adaptive competence would be the same in both contexts.

Attachment relationships are maintained by both partners (Sroufe and Fleeson, 1986). In this study, we examined the social behaviors directed by children toward their caregivers. It is not clear how the caregivers, mothers or teachers, responded to and supported these behaviors. The quality of children's relationships with mothers is related to maternal sensitivity and responsivity (Ainsworth, Blehar, Waters, and Wall, 1978). Patterns of attachment with teachers are also associated with levels of involvement and sensitivity (Howes and Hamilton, 1992a; Whitebrook, Howes, and Phillips, 1990). Teacher sensitivity and the quality of the interactions that they have with children are also related to overall child care quality issues such as levels of education and training, child-teacher ratios, and group size (Whitebrook, Howes, and Phillips, 1990). Overall, the relationships that teachers form with children may be related to these quality issues. However, teachers do not form identical attachment relationships with every child in their care (Goossens and Van IJzendoorn, 1990; Sakai and Howes, 1991), nor are the attachment relationships children have with their mothers and teachers necessarily concordant (Goossens and Van IJzendoorn, 1990). In exploring the development of attachment relationships between children and their day-care teachers, we need to focus not only on the overall quality variables that influence teacher and child behavior but also on the individual differences of teachers and children that lead to the development of different patterns of social relationships.

References

Ainslie, R. C., and Anderson, C. W. "Day Care Children's Relationships to Their Mothers and Caregivers: An Inquiry into the Conditions for Development of Attachment." In R. C. Ainslie (ed.), *The Child and the Day Care Setting: Qualitative Variations and Development*. New York: Praeger, 1984.

Ainsworth, M.D.S., Blehar, M. C., Waters, E., and Wall, S. *Patterns of Attachment: A Psychological Study of the Strange Situation*. Hillsdale, N.J.: Erlbaum, 1978.

Blanchard, M., and Main, M. "Avoidance of the Attachment Figure and Social-Emotional Adjustment in Day Care Infants." *Developmental Psychology*, 1979, *15*, 445–446.

Bowlby, J. *Attachment and Loss*. Vol. 1: *Attachment*. (Rev. ed.) New York: Basic Books, 1982.

Bretherton, I. "New Perspectives on Attachment Relations: Security, Communication, and Internal Working Models." In J. D. Osofsky (ed.), *Handbook of Infant Development*. New York: Wiley, 1987.

Goossens, F. A., and Van IJzendoorn, M. H. "Quality of Infants' Attachment to Professional Caregivers: Relation to Infant-Parent Attachment and Daycare Characteristics." *Child Development*, 1990, *61*, 832–837.

Harms, T., and Clifford, R. *Early Childhood Environmental Rating Scale*. New York: Teachers College Press, 1980.

Howes, C., and Hamilton, C. E. "Children's Relationships with Caregivers: Mothers and Child Care Teachers." *Child Development*, 1992a, *63*, 859–866.

Howes, C., and Hamilton, C. E. "Children's Relationships with Child Care Teachers: Stability and Concordance with Parental Attachments." *Child Development*, 1992b, *63*, 867–878.

Howes, C., Rodning, C., Galluzzo, D., and Myers, L. "Attachment and Child Care: Relationships with Mother and Caregiver." *Early Childhood Research Quarterly*, 1988, *3*, 403–416.

Howes, C., and others. "Social Relationships with Adults and Peers Within Child Care and Families." Paper presented at the biennial meeting of the Society for Research in Child Development. Kansas City, Missouri, April 1990.

Lamb, M. E., Thompson, R. A., Gardner, W. P., and Charnov, E. L. *Infant-Mother Attachment: The Origins and Developmental Significance of Individual Differences in Strange Situation Behavior*. Hillsdale, N.J.: Erlbaum, 1985.

Oppenheim, D., Sagi, A., and Lamb, M. E. "Infant-Adult Attachments in the Kibbutz and Their Relation to Socioemotional Development 4 Years Later." *Developmental Psychology*, 1988, *24*, 427–433.

Pianta, R. C., and Nimetz, S. L. "Relationships Between Children and Teachers: Associations with Classroom and Home Behavior." *Journal of Applied Developmental Psychology*, 1991, *12*, 379–393.

Ragozin, A. S. "Attachment Behavior of Day Care Children: Naturalistic and Laboratory Observations." *Child Development,* 1980, *51,* 409–415.

Sakai, L. M., and Howes, C. "Quality of Attachment: (Dis)Similarity Between Two Children and the Same Caregiver." Unpublished manuscript, University of California, Los Angeles, 1991.

Sroufe, L. A. "Infant-Caregiver Attachment and Patterns of Adaptation in Preschool: The Roots of Maladaptation and Competence." In M. Perlmutter (ed.), *Minnesota Symposia on Child Psychology.* Vol. 16. Hillsdale, N.J.: Erlbaum, 1983.

Sroufe, L. A., and Fleeson, J. "Attachment and the Construction of Relationships." In W. Hartup and Z. Rubin (eds.), *Relationships and Development.* Hillsdale, N.J.: Erlbaum, 1986.

Sroufe, L. A., and Waters, E. "Attachment as an Organizational Construct." *Child Development,* 1977, *48,* 1184–1199.

Waters, E., and Deane, K. E. "Defining and Assessing Individual Differences in Attachment Relationships: Q-Methodology and the Organization of Behavior in Infancy and Early Childhood." In I. Bretherton and E. Waters (eds.), *Growing Points of Attachment: Theory and Research.* Monographs of the Society for Research in Child Development, vol. 50, nos. 1–2 (serial no. 209). Chicago: University of Chicago Press, 1985.

Waters, E., Wippman, J., and Sroufe, L. A. "Attachment, Positive Affect, and Competence in the Peer Group: Two Studies in Construct Validation." *Child Development,* 1979, *50,* 821–829.

Whitebrook, M., Howes, C., and Phillips, D. A. *Who Cares? Child Care Teachers and the Quality of Care in America.* Final Report of the National Child Care Staffing Study. Oakland, Calif.: Child Care Employee Project, 1990.

CLAIRE E. HAMILTON is a doctoral student in the Graduate School of Education, University of California, Los Angeles. Her research focuses on young children's development of social relationships and continuity of attachment from infancy through adolescence.

CAROLLEE HOWES is professor, Graduate School of Education, University of California, Los Angeles. Her research interests include development of social relationships and social communication with adults and peers.

Child-teacher relationships show wide-ranging patterns based on affective valence and engagement and are a unique part of school adjustment.

Teacher-Child Relationships and the Process of Adjusting to School

Robert C. Pianta, Michael Steinberg

Research on teacher-child relationships is based on two foundations: (1) the common experience of teachers, parents, and children that the child's relationship with his or her teacher is an especially important component of the school experience and related to child adjustment and (2) research in social development, attachment theory, and teaching and learning that increasingly shows the importance of adult-child relationships as contexts for development. The present study blends theory on child-adult attachment with research on the importance of early school experiences in determining the trajectories of children's school progress (Sroufe, 1989). Currently, there is a noticeable lack of theory regarding the processes by which children move from the home or day-care context to the school context and the factors that relate to this transition and determine adjustment in school. Moreover, as a society faced with enormous rates of school failure, attention to new forms of inquiry into school adjustment may lead to policies and practices that attenuate the social risk associated with high rates of early school failure.

Alexander and Entwisle (1988) argue that few school experiences after third grade have enough weight to alter the already established course of achievement. Research on preschool children indicates that an important element of adjusting to school is a relationship with a teacher that serves the child's development and education (Sroufe, 1983). In previous work (Pianta and Nimetz, 1991; Pianta and Steinberg, 1991), we have shown that patterns of teacher-child relationships in kindergar-

Preparation of this chapter was supported by the Commonwealth Center for the Education of Teachers, University of Virginia and James Madison University.

ten (for example, conflicted, open/close, and dependent) are related to behavior in the home and are predictive of subsequent school adjustment. Erickson and Pianta (1989) suggest that parent-child attachment patterns are closely linked with how the child negotiates the social and academic demands of school, via the representational models of self, other, and relationships that mediate experience and are transferred across contexts. Although teacher-child relationships may have tremendous impact in altering the course of school adjustment (Pederson, Faucher, and Eaton, 1978), they have not been subjected to any systematic empirical research. Studies of teacher-child relationships could be important tests of theories suggesting coherence and stability in relationships (Sroufe, 1983). However, most studies documenting the positive impact of the teacher-child relationship are case reports (Pederson, Faucher, and Eaton, 1978) or comments on high-risk populations (Garmezy, 1984; Werner and Smith, 1982). Issues examined in this chapter include the role that relationships between children and parents and children and teachers play in determining school adjustment, factors influencing adult-child relationships, and measurement issues addressed in pilot research.

Relationships with Adults and Children's School Adjustment: Parents

Research on parent-child relationships and child competence provides conceptual and methodological background for studying teacher-child relationships. The parent-child relationship data provide a compelling rationale for the influence of adult-child relationships on child adjustment as well as a framework and method of inquiry. Child attachment to caregivers is linked with peer relations, problem solving, and school adjustment (for example, Bus and Van IJzendoorn, 1988; Greenberg and Speltz, 1988; Sroufe, 1989). Bus and Van IJzendoorn (1988) demonstrated linkages between emergent literacy skills, mother-child interaction, and security of child-mother attachment in a sample of children one and one-half to five and one-half years of age. Securely attached children attended to their mothers, required less discipline, received more instruction, engaged in more spontaneous reading, and performed better on emergent literacy measures than did insecurely attached children. Sroufe (1983) indicated that children with a history of insecure attachment elicited rejection from peers and adults in preschool and had difficulty in learning. Mother-child interaction in the preschool years predicts referral for special education, classroom behavior problems, and academic achievement (Erickson, Sroufe, and Egeland, 1985; Lewis, Feiring, McGuffog, and Jaskir, 1984; Pianta and others, 1990). As a group, these studies clearly indicate the importance of adult-child relationships in social and learning processes critical to early school adjustment. Moreover, they suggest continuity and stability between parent-child relationships and aspects of school adjustment. In a study of four-year-old children, Nimetz (1992) indicates that dimensions of affect and control in the parent-child dyad are highly predictive of security and dependence in the teacher-child relationship, and of social adjustment in the kindergarten classroom two years later.

Relationships with Adults and Children's School Adjustment: Teachers

The teacher-child relationship, especially in the primary grades, is a potential target for patterns of child behavior, beliefs, and feelings previously developed within the context of the parent-child attachment relationship (Erickson and Pianta, 1989). Experiences with caregivers influence patterns of expectations of self and others and feelings of self-worth, trust, and motivation that are brought to interactions with a teacher. However, little is known about continuity in these processes across the home-school transition and what factors influence continuity and discontinuity. For example, is having a teacher who responds in a manner similar to the primary caregiver related to stability in relationship patterns (Sroufe, 1989)? In an investigation conducted within our laboratory, Nimetz (1992) observed parent-child interaction and assessed teacher-child relationships using an adaptation of the Waters and Deane (1985) Q-Set. There was considerable support for continuity across parent-child and teacher-child relationships. Continuity was indicated when the degree to which parent-child dyads shared affective experience (the child openly sharing emotion with the parent that was accepted by the parent) predicted teachers' reports of a secure relationship. Parent-child dyads that had not resolved issues of control (parental over- or undercontrol) predicted teacher-child relationships marked by dependence and conflict. These data suggest that child experiences in close relationships with a parent, particularly experiences around expression of emotion and regulation of behavior, are predictive of the ways in which the child relates to teachers.

Teachers' responses to child-initiated relationship behaviors also appear influential in determining classroom adjustment. Pederson, Faucher, and Eaton (1978), in a case report on a first-grade teacher, provide data on the impact of a teacher who formed relationships with students that, according to their reports, made them feel worthwhile, supported their independence, motivated them to achieve, and provided them with support to interpret and cope with environmental demands. This teacher's students differed from their same-age peers on dropout rates, academic achievement, behavioral competence, and adjustment in the adult world. The relation between felt security in a relationship with an adult and freedom to explore the world in a competent manner is a hallmark of the parent-child attachment relationship and appears also to operate within the teacher-child relationship, according to Pederson, Faucher, and Eaton's data. In the child-parent attachment process, sensitivity by the parent (for example, reading child cues and responding contingently and warmly) is a major determinant of security. We know almost nothing about teacher behaviors that relate to the kinds of relationships described by Pederson, Faucher, and Eaton. Furthermore, the study of teacher-child relationships may have wider policy implications for wide-scale efforts to attenuate societal risk related to early school failure as teacher-child relationships are often viewed as important components of successful interventions. Werner and Smith (1982) studied a poverty sample and determined that one of the factors accounting for positive outcomes among these high-risk children was a supportive relationship with a teacher. These relationships prevented many of the outcomes (for example, dropping out, behavior problems and psychopathology, academic failure) that plague American schools today. Boyer (1983) notes that a relationship with a supportive teacher is a major factor associated with prevention of dropouts. The social and relational nature of risk is underscored by the backgrounds of students who fail in school. These students often have experienced considerable relationship stress, such as parental divorce, child maltreatment, parental depression. Healthy teacher-child relationships appear to help ameliorate the negative consequences of these experiences. Empirical work describing teacher-child relationships, documenting their benefits, and linking types of teacher-child relationships to child, teacher, school, and contextual factors is the next step in harnessing this powerful influence on children's school outcomes. Moreover, the extent to which teacher-child relationships have an ameliorative effect on children's representational models of self, other, and relationships has implications for theories about the continuity of these representations and the factors influencing discontinuity.

Measurement Issues

Teachers' attributions, interactions with children, expectations, and attitudes are associated with children's classroom adjustment (Alexander and Entwisle, 1988; Brophy and Good, 1974; Pederson, Faucher, and Eaton, 1978). Children's feelings about teachers, time spent in contact with teachers, and attentiveness to teacher-directed activities have also been related to school success (Minuchin and Shapiro, 1983). Most of this research has been driven by a behavioral psychology paradigm that has limited the methods used for studying teachers and children, and the interpretations of the data have often been narrowed to instructional or disciplinary strategies. Therefore, little theory exists that integrates social, affective, and learning processes within the medium of classroom interactions between children and teachers. The study of relationships encompasses interactive behaviors and individual cognitive, affective, and motivational attributes (Hinde and Stevenson-Hinde, 1987; Waters and Sroufe, 1983) and may contribute to developing theories about how these processes are integrated in the context of the classroom. Development of valid measures of teacher-child relationships is one step in this process.

Pilot investigations by our research group include studies to validate instruments for measuring teacher-child relationships: (1) a teacher self-report measure (the Student-Teacher Relationship Scale (STRS); Pianta, 1990), (2) a teacher Q-Sort measure, (3) an observational measure used by outside observers in the classroom (Relationship Observation System; Pianta, 1991), and (4) a standardized laboratory observation procedure to assess teacher-child interaction in a problem-solving situation and teacher-child attachment (Nimetz, 1992). This chapter focuses on results derived from a large-scale use of the STRS.

Methods

This study was designed to gain information from kindergarten teachers regarding their relationships with each of the children in their classes and the children's classroom behavior.

Sample. The sample consisted of 436 children and 26 of their kindergarten teachers. This was the entire kindergarten population of a small city school district and there were no exclusion criteria. The mean age of the children in the sample was five years three months (range = four years five months to six years six months). There were 205 boys and 231 girls in the sample. The sample was 65 percent white, 31 percent black, and 4 percent Asian. The education of the children's mothers was distributed as follows: 5 percent below eighth grade, 15 percent some high school, 27 percent high school graduate, 16 percent some college, 9 percent college graduate, 6 percent master's degree, and 3 percent doctoral degree. As a group, the teachers averaged 10.3 years of teaching experience, ranging from 0 to 20 years.

Measures and Procedures. Teachers completed a scale that measures children's classroom behavior, and parents completed an additional behavior checklist. In addition, information was obtained on children's cognitive ability.

Student-Teacher Relationship Scale (STRS). The STRS is a thirty-one-item rating scale, using a Likert-type format, designed to assess teachers' perceptions of their relationships with particular students. Teachers completed the STRS in May of the kindergarten year for each of the children in their classrooms. The items on this scale were based on items included in a previous sixteen-item version of the scale (Pianta and Nimetz, 1991). Items were based on behaviors derived from attachment theory, the Attachment Q-Set (Waters and Deane, 1985), and a review of literature on teacher-child interactions. The items were intended to tap teachers' representational models of their relationships with students and therefore to involve the teacher's feelings and beliefs about her relationship with a student and her feelings and beliefs about the student's behavior toward her. Items were selected to assess dimensions of warmth/security, anger/dependence, and anxiety/insecurity. Items assessing security include "This student trusts me" and "I share a warm, affectionate relationship with this student." Items assessing insecurity include "This child seems wary of me" and "This child constantly needs reassurance from me."

In the pilot study with seventy-two children using the sixteen-item version, three factors were derived: secure, improved, and dependent. Alpha reliability for the total scale was .85, and alphas for the factor-based subscales exceeded .60. In the pilot study, there were no differences in scores of boys and girls. Significant associations were obtained between the pilot STRS security scores and competence behaviors at home and in kindergarten and first-grade classrooms. Pilot STRS dependence scores were associated with acting-out behaviors at home and school, and improved scores were related to positive behavior problems at the start of kindergarten and subsequent positive adjustment in first grade. Analysis of these data from the sixteen-item pilot STRS supported further study, using an expanded form of the STRS, of the possible role that teacher-child relationships play in children's school adjustment.

Preschool Behavior Rating Scale (PBRS). At school entry, each child's mother completed the PBRS (Caldwell and Pianta, 1991), a forty-four-item behavior rating scale using a 4-point Likert-type format. Three subscale scores were derived from factor analysis: competence, acting out, and internalizing, along with a total score. Internal consistency reliabilities were .83 for the total scale, .78 for competence, .75 for acting out, and .72 for internalizing. These subscales as well as the total score were each significant predictors of teachers' decisions to retain children in kindergarten and were associated with patterns of mother-child interaction (Caldwell and Pianta, 1991).

Teacher-Child Rating Scale (TCRS). The TCRS (Hightower and others, 1986) is a thirty-eight-item teacher-report rating scale of children's social, behavioral, and academic competence and problems. The items on the Problem Behaviors scale load on three factor-based subscales: conduct, learning, and shy-anxious problems. The items on the Competence scale load on four factor-based subscales: frustration tolerance, work habits, assertive social skills, and peer social skills. Internal consistency reliabilities on these scales exceeded .90, and test-retest reliability exceeded .80 across three samples. Both the Problem Behaviors and the Competence scales are highly correlated with the Child Behavior Checklist (Hightower and others, 1986). The TCRS was completed by all kindergarten teachers for each child in their classrooms in November and May, and by all first-grade teachers, for all children, in March of first grade.

Stanford-Binet Fourth Edition (SBFE). A two-subtest short form (vocabulary and bead memory) of the SBFE was used as a general estimate of child intelligence. These subtests are highly correlated with the general intelligence factor and are recommended for screening purposes.

Retention in Kindergarten. Each year, kindergarten teachers made decisions to retain children in kindergarten. The school district was making a purposeful effort to reduce the number of retention decisions during the years in which this study was conducted, 1988 and 1989. Teachers made these decisions based on a number of factors, including social behaviors, academic readiness skills, and perceptions of general maturity and peer relations. These decisions were made in May of the kindergarten year, approximately two weeks after the STRS was administered. There were forty-seven children retained.

Data Analyses. The thirty-one-item revised STRS was factor analyzed using Varimax rotation in order to examine the dimensions of teacher-child relationships assessed by the STRS. Internal consistency reliabilities were performed on the total STRS scale and subscales derived from the factor analysis. In order to examine the relations between teachers' perceptions of their relationships with students and the students' behaviors at home and in the classroom, correlations were computed between the STRS subscales and subscales from the TCRS and PBRS. The role of teacher-child relationships in buffering or exacerbating risk for retention was also examined in a series of analyses. Finally, a descriptive typology of teacher-child relationships was explored in a cluster analysis.

Results

The results indicate considerable variability in teachers' reports of relationships with students, and in associations between child-teacher relationships and children's classroom behavior, on the one hand, and teachers' decisions to retain children in kindergarten, on the other.

Factor Analysis and Internal Consistency. Factor analysis of the STRS resulted in five factors accounting for 3 percent of the variance: conflicted/angry, warm/close, open, dependent, and troubled/closed. The results of the factor analysis are presented in Table 4.1.

The first factor, conflicted/angry, accounted for 30.4 percent of the

Table 4.1. Factor Analysis of Student-Teacher Relationship Scale

Items	Rotated Factor Matrix				
	Conflicted	Warm	Open	Dependent	Troubled
Affectionate, warm	-.45	.57	.21	-.13	-.26
Struggling	.76	.21	.04	.11	.16
If upset, seeks comfort	-.23	.64	.31	-.28	-.05
Uncomfortable with touch	.10	-.67	.08	-.04	.19
Values relationship	-.34	.64	.24	-.15	-.12
Hurt/embarrassed if corrected	.06	-.10	.05	.13	-.05
Does not accept help	.24	.21	-.05	.02	.57
Praised, beams with pride	.03	.70	.10	.02	.05
Reacts to separation	.02	.01	.16	.78	.27
Shares information	.03	.19	.87	-.05	.09
Overly dependent	.12	-.15	.11	.81	.02
Easily angered	.77	.12	-.04	.04	.28
Tries to please	-.37	.49	.30	-.07	.18
Feels treated unfairly	.75	.11	.02	-.05	.04
Asks for help, not needed	.38	-.13	-.11	.49	-.28
Easy to tune in feelings	.11	.33	.71	.10	-.02
Source of punishment	.69	.20	-.01	.01	-.05
Expresses hurt/ jealousy	.60	-.22	.01	.39	-.00
Remains angry/ resistant	.81	.02	.05	-.07	.11
Responds well to look/voice	.56	.27	.13	.02	.09
Drains my energy	.79	.11	.08	.15	.15
Copying behavior	-.06	.50	.15	-.07	.09
Bad mood, difficult day	.79	.15	-.02	.09	.19
Unpredictable feelings	.76	.16	.05	.03	.23
Uncomfortable with child	.60	.26	.22	.25	.01
Often think about child	.32	-.22	.23	.14	.60
Whines or cries	.56	-.02	-.08	.37	-.19
Sneaky/manipulative	.74	.06	.03	.06	-.08
Openly shares feelings	-.02	.25	.85	-.11	.01
Feel effective and confident	-.46	.52	.24	.20	-.14
Eigenvalue	9.12	4.10	1.78	1.26	1.14
Percentage variance	30.40	13.70	5.90	4.30	3.80
Alpha reliability	.93	.84	.83	.64	1.53

Note: N = 436

variance and was loaded on most heavily by items assessing child anger at the teacher, the teacher's feelings of being emotionally drained by the relationship with the student, and a feeling that the teacher was always struggling with the student. The second factor, warm/close, accounted for 14.1 percent of the variance and was loaded on by items assessing the child's expression of positive affect in interactions with the teacher and items reflecting teacher feelings of warmth and closeness toward the student. The third factor, open, accounted for 7 percent of the variance and reflected open communication between child and teacher. It was loaded on most heavily by items measuring the extent to which the child shared personal information with the teacher and the teacher's feelings of being in tune with the child's feelings. The fourth factor, dependent, accounted for 3 percent of the variance and reflected the child's strong reactions to separation from the teacher and frequent, unnecessary requests for the teacher's help. The fifth factor, troubled/closed, accounted for 1 percent of the variance and indicated the child's refusal to accept the teacher's help when offered, and the teacher's report of being preoccupied with their relationship with the child when away from work.

Coefficient alpha for the total thirty-one-item STRS was .90. Alpha for the twelve-item conflicted/angry subscale was .93, .84 for the eight-item warm/close subscale, .83 for the three-item open subscale, .64 for the two-item dependent subscale, and .53 for the two-item troubled/closed subscale.

Correlations between the STRS subscales and the PBRS (parent report) subscales are reported in Table 4.2. These correlations indicate a low-to-moderate association between teachers' perceptions of their relationships with students and parents' reports of the students' behaviors at home. Acting-out behavior at home was associated with teacher relationships characterized by conflict and closed communication. Teacher-child relationships characterized by open communication were negatively associated with parents' reports of child anxiety. Children described as

Table 4.2. Correlations Between STRS and PBRS

STRS Subscales	PBRS Subscales			
	Acting Out	Anxious	Competent	Total
Conflicted	.29[a]	.04	-.15[a]	-.15[a]
Warm	-.07	-.07	.18[a]	-.18[a]
Open	.03	-.21[a]	.23[a]	-.26[a]
Dependent	.02	.07	.05	-.07
Troubled	.16[a]	.05	.03	-.04
Total	-.25[a]	-.01	.19[a]	-.19[a]

Note: STRS = Student-Teacher Relationship Scale, PBRS = Preschool Behavior Rating Scale.
[a] $p < .01$

competent at home had relationships with teachers characterized by openness and a lack of conflict.

Correlations among the STRS and TCRS measures of teachers' perceptions of the children's classroom behavior in the fall term of kindergarten are reported in Table 4.3. The correlations were mostly significant and in the moderate range. Children rated in the fall as having conduct problems were reported to have conflicted and dependent relationships lacking warmth and open communication. Internalizing behavior problems in the fall were related to lack of open communication; learning problems predicted conflict and dependence. Child competence in the classroom predicted positive teacher-child relationships. Frustration tolerance correlated negatively with conflict, dependence, and troubled scores from the STRS, as did the work habits score from the TCRS. Social skills on the TCRS correlated negatively with conflict and positively with close and open.

Correlations between the TCRS and subsequent behavior in the first-grade classroom are reported in Table 4.4. The correlations indicate the same pattern of moderate association between teacher relationships in kindergarten and subsequent classroom behavior rated by a different teacher in first grade.

Analyses also were performed to examine the role of teacher-child relationships in kindergarten teachers' decisions to retain children. The children retained in kindergarten were compared with a sample of nonretained peers matched for teacher and age. Univariate t-test analyses, using Bonferroni correction, are reported in Table 4.5. Relative to their nonretained peers in the same classroom, relationships between teachers and retained children were more conflicted and troubled and less warm and open. In a multivariate analysis of variance controlling for the kindergarten teachers' ratings of the children's behavior in the classroom (measured concurrently with the STRS), there was a significant overall effect for retention (Wilk's lambda = .95, F = 3.85, p < .001), with univariate follow-up tests indicating that retained children had more conflicted and less warm relationships than did the nonretained children after controlling for classroom behavior.

Predictions of retention decisions were made using data collected during the kindergarten-entry screening process (SBFE subtests, McCarthy Tests of Children's Abilities motor scales, the Fluharty Preschool Language Screening Test, and the PBRS subscales). With these measures entered stepwise in a discriminant function analysis with retention status (retained, nonretained) as the dependent measure, 77.7 percent of the children were correctly classified. Seventy-six percent of those children actually promoted were predicted to be promoted, while 24.3 percent were predicted to be retained (false positives). Seven percent of the children actually retained were predicted to be promoted (false negatives), while 92.7 percent were predicted to be retained.

Table 4.3. Correlations Between STRS and Kindergarten Fall-Term TCRS

				TCRS Subscales				
STRS Subscales	Behavior Problems	Conduct Problems	Internalizing	Learning Problems	Competence	Frustration Tolerance	Work Habits	Social Skills
Conflicted	.51	.67	-.02	.47	-.51	-.59	-.39	-.39
Warm	-.37	-.31	-.27	-.26	.29	.24	.22	.32
Open	-.27	.03	-.42	-.19	.23	.07	.23	.33
Dependent	.26	.22	.11	.29	-.31	-.31	-.26	-.22
Troubled	.22	.31	-.03	-.23	-.32	-.38	-.25	-.24
Total	-.57	-.61	-.20	-.50	.56	.57	.43	.48

Note: All r's, $p < .01$; STRS = Student-Teacher Relationship Scale, TCRS = Teacher-Child Rating Scale.

Table 4.4. Correlations Between STRS and First-Grade TCRS

				TCRS Subscales				
STRS Subscales	Behavior Problems	Conduct Problems	Internalizing	Learning Problems	Competence	Frustration Tolerance	Work Habits	Social Skills
Conflicted	.53	.61	.17	.46	-.43	-.51	-.39	-.40
Warm	-.32	-.29	-.18	-.30	.25	.18	.20	.27
Open	-.19	.03	-.29	-.18	.25	.06	.18	.27
Dependent	.24	.20	.15	.24	-.20	-.23	-.19	-.14
Troubled	.33	.30	.19	.31	-.26	-.28	-.23	-.27
Total	-.56	-.56	-.26	-.50	.46	.47	.41	.44

Note: All *r*'s ≥ .18, *p* < .01; STRS = Student-Teacher Relationship Scale, TCRS = Teacher-Child Rating Scale.

In this analysis, we compared the children who were predicted to be retained but *not* actually retained (*N* = 65) with those children predicted to be retained and actually retained (*N* = 38) on the STRS total and subscales. The results of these comparisons are presented in Table 4.6. Children who were predicted to be retained in kindergarten but were actually promoted had relationships with their kindergarten teachers that were characterized as more warm, open, and less troubled than did children predicted to be retained and actually retained. The groups differed on the total STRS score, indicating a trend toward more positive relationships in the group that was eventually promoted.

In an exploratory analysis, we examined the role of teacher-child relationships in decisions to retain children who, on the basis of standardized tests, were predicted to be promoted. This group of children was very small (*N* = 3); therefore we did not perform any statistical tests in comparisons with other groups. Group means indicated that this group of children had highly negative relationships with their teachers.

Table 4.5. Comparisons of Retained Versus Nonretained Children on STRS

	Retained		Nonretained			
	X	*SD*	*X*	*SD*	*t*	*p*
Conflicted	53.10	11.23	49.44	10.90	2.12	.035
Warm	32.11	5.35	30.09	5.12	2.50	.012
Open	9.46	2.88	91.59	3.47	4.02	.000
Dependent	11.57	2.55	11.84	2.42	.68	.500
Troubled	7.54	1.86	6.83	2.01	2.46	.025

Note: Retained *N* = 47, nonretained *N* = 50.

Table 4.6. Comparisons of Predicted Retention/Promotion and Predicted Retention/Retention Groups on STRS Subscales

STRS Subscales	Predicted Retention but Promoted		Predicted Retention and Retained		*F*
	X	*SD*	*X*	*SD*	
Conflicted	51.38	10.78	50.05	10.40	.62
Warm	32.83	4.50	30.13	5.24	2.65[a]
Open	11.29	2.44	9.45	3.71	2.74[a]
Dependent	11.09	2.38	11.47	2.59	−.74
Troubled	6.78	2.01	7.82	1.74	−2.62[a]
STRS total	117.37	15.63	111.08	15.97	1.94

[a] $p < .01$

The mean score for the conflicted/angry subscale for the three children predicted to be promoted but actually retained was ten points higher than for the group of children predicted to be retained and actually retained. The mean scores of these two groups on all other STRS subscales were within three points of each other, suggesting that conflict between child and teacher was a distinguishing feature of this group.

A final set of analyses described categories of teacher-child relationships as viewed by the teacher in a cluster analysis of the teachers' responses to the STRS. The cluster procedure was performed on the five factor-based subscales described earlier and employed Ward's method. A six-group solution was obtained. The first group, dependent ($N = 47$), was moderately conflicted, lacking warmth, very high on dependency, and average on the other scales. The second group, positively involved ($N = 171$), was low on conflict/anger, high on warmth and open communication, and moderately dependent. The third group, angry ($N = 20$) was very high on conflict; low on warmth, open communication, and dependence; and high on the troubled dimension. The fourth group, functional ($N = 154$), was average on all scales. The fifth group, angry/dependent ($N = 12$), was very high on conflict, dependence, and troubled. The sixth group, uninvolved ($N = 32$) was very low on open communication, and low on conflict, warmth, and dependence.

Discussion

This study began systematic inquiry into the relationships that children form with their kindergarten teachers and the possible role that these relationships play in school adjustment. The STRS is a teacher self-report rating scale containing items related to teachers' feelings and beliefs about their relationships with students and the students' behavior toward them, and ratings of students' relationship-oriented behaviors. The STRS was designed to assess teachers' internal working models of relationships (Bretherton, 1985), with the hypothesis that these models may ultimately guide teacher behavior with students in meaningful ways, and that individual differences in teachers' internal working models are systematically related to individual differences in children's behavior and the children's other relationships with adults. The data analyses indicated that (1) descriptive patterns of teachers' relationships with students as assessed by the STRS are conceptually similar to patterns of child-parent attachment (Cassidy and Marvin, 1991; Greenberg, Cicchetti, and Cummings, 1990; Main and Cassidy, 1988), (2) teacher-child relationships are predictably related to, but not redundant with, child behavior at home and school, and (3) teachers' internal working models of their relationships with students contribute to an understanding of children's adjustments in school.

What Patterns of Teacher-Child Relationships Emerge from Teachers' Perceptions? The factor analysis and cluster analysis data address this issue. From the factor analysis, several dimensions of teacher-child relationships emerged that were very similar to dimensions along which child-parent attachment relationships are classified using the system for two-and-one-half- to four-year-old children (Cassidy and Marvin, 1991), especially affect and engagement. The emotional experience of the student and teacher was a central dimension along which relationships appeared differentiated; conflict/anger and warmth were the first two factors that emerged. A dimension of involvement was evident in the open communication, dependent, and troubled factors, each reflecting a different type of involvement (or its absence) between child and teacher. The patterns of relationships revealed by the cluster analyses indicated how different types of affect and involvement were organized. Child-teacher involvement was the primary dimension around which the dependent and uninvolved clusters were organized. The angry cluster was organized primarily around negative affect. The positively involved and angry/dependent clusters combined affect and involvement. The functional group combined moderate levels of affect and involvement. The set of clusters resulting from this analysis is presented in Figure 4.1.

The angry/dependent and angry clusters are conceptually similar, and similar in terms of child behaviors (for example, manipulation) to the dependence dimension of child-parent attachment described by Waters and Deane's (1985) Attachment Q-Set. Avoidance is evident in the description of the uninvolved cluster, especially the tendency of the child to be markedly uncommunicative about personal information and to move away from dependence (Cassidy and Marvin, 1991; Main and Cassidy, 1988; Waters and Deane, 1985). The positively involved group of children showed behaviors toward their teachers that indicated secure relationships; they shared personal information and appeared comfortable with dependence, but were not too dependent, and they displayed positive affect in response to the teachers' interactions or in regard to their relationships with the teachers (Cassidy and Marvin, 1991; Main and Cassidy, 1988).

Are Teacher-Child Relationships Related to Child Behavior? The data clearly support the view that teacher-child relationships are related to child behavior at home and in the classroom (Pianta and Nimetz, 1991). Continuity from child behavior at home to child behavior in relation to teachers was indicated by the low-to-moderate relations between the STRS and parent report measure. Children who were reported to have problems with acting-out behaviors at home formed conflicted relationships with teachers; children viewed as competent by their parents had warm and open relationships with teachers, and anxious children at home were rated low on open communication with teachers. Support for

Figure 4.1. Conceptual Scheme for Patterns of Teacher-Child Relationships on Affect and Involvement Dimensions

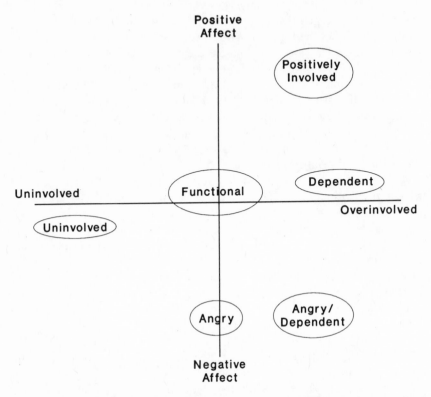

continuity is evident in the differential validity of these relations, and each of these relations indicates consistency in underlying patterns of relating toward adults that are carried from home to school (Sroufe, 1989; Sroufe and Fleeson, 1986).

Once in school, it is clear that the child's classroom behavior played a major role in the formation of the teacher impressions assessed by the STRS, as would be predicted by theories of relationship formation (Hinde and Stevenson-Hinde, 1987). The correlations linking the children's classroom behavior in November of kindergarten with the STRS in May were moderate, but not as high as the test-retest correlations for the classroom behavior measure, and certainly not high enough to consider the STRS redundant with classroom behavior. The highest of the correlations indicate that conduct problems in the classroom predict conflicted teacher-child relationships. Low internalizing scores predicted an open relationship, and social skills were related to warm, open relationships with the kindergarten teachers. Again, these correlations are consistent with theoretical perspectives that relationships build on behaviors and interactions (Hinde and Stevenson-Hinde, 1987). It is noteworthy that the patterns of correlations between kindergarten classroom behavior and the STRS were replicated in the correlations between the STRS and first-grade classroom behavior; the relations between child classroom behavior and teacher-child relationships found for kindergarten teachers were not solely a function of the same rater (the kindergarten teacher) and supported the idea that children bring with them patterns of relating to adults and replicate these across contexts (Sroufe and Fleeson, 1986).

Teacher-Child Relationships and Understanding the Process of Adjusting to School. Schooling is a largely social process in the early years. Markers of educational failure are usually measures of social processes; retention in kindergarten can be considered an example. The data suggest that a teacher's decision to retain a student in kindergarten is not solely a function of that child's classroom behavior or ability but instead involves the teacher's perceptions and feelings about his or her relationship with that student. Furthermore, the data suggest that teacher-child relationships (as assessed through the teacher's perspective) act as protective factors for children who otherwise would be predicted to suffer from this form of failure in the early grades. Children who were predicted to be retained but were not actually retained had more positive relationships with teachers than did those who were retained. As many authors have indicated, positive relationships between a high-risk child and an adult can serve to alter that child's vulnerability and response to risk and enhance resilience (Garmezy, 1984; Rutter, 1987). The educational policy implications of these data, if replicated, are substantial and could affect decisions to place students with certain teachers, as well as training for teachers of young children, and support efforts to enhance teacher-child relationships through low student-teacher ratios and nongraded classrooms and schools.

Directions for Future Research

This research represents an effort to integrate research and theories of children's social development with social processes in early educational contexts. Attachment theory provides a strong conceptual base for this bridge to educational applications, and the data suggest that relationships between teachers and children may be a fruitful topic of research on continuity in development and the role of relationships as superordinate regulators of individual differences in children (Sameroff, 1989). There are a number of directions for future research to consider. First, there is a need for attention to measurement issues in this research. This chapter presents results of a self-report paper-and-pencil measure; this is clearly not the optimal type of measure for assessing relationships (Hinde and Stevenson-Hinde, 1987). Observational studies of classroom interactions over numerous occasions, informed by attachment theory, can provide the descriptive base necessary for further development of ideas about teacher-child relationships and their functions. Further research linking child-parent attachment (as assessed with the Strange Situation) with observations of teacher-child relationships can provide information on specific dimensions of continuity and coherence across these two relational contexts. Work in our laboratory suggests that dimensions of affect and control are preserved across child-parent and child-teacher relationships (Nimetz, 1992). Finally, close study of the developmental and educational outcomes of children who experience a wide variety of relational contexts (risk/no risk, stable/unstable) can highlight the contribution of work on teacher-child relationships to theories of vulnerability and resilience (Rutter, 1987) and provide an empirical basis for innovative educational strategies such as nongraded classrooms.

References

Alexander, K., and Entwisle, D. *Achievement in the First Two Years of School.* Monographs of the Society for Research in Child Development, vol. 53 (serial no. 218). Chicago: University of Chicago Press, 1988.

Boyer, E. *High School: A Report on Secondary Education in America.* New York: HarperCollins, 1983.

Bretherton, I. "Attachment Theory: Retrospect and Prospect." In I. Bretherton and E. Waters (eds.), *Growing Points of Attachment: Theory and Research.* Monographs of the Society for Research in Child Development, vol. 50, nos. 1–2 (serial no. 209). Chicago: University of Chicago Press, 1985.

Brophy, J. E., and Good, T. L. *Teacher-Student Relationships: Causes and Consequences.* Troy, Mo.: Holt, Rinehart & Winston, 1974.

Bus, A. G., and Van IJzendoorn, M. H. "Mother-Child Interactions, Attachment, and Emergent Literacy: A Cross-Sectional Study." *Child Development,* 1988, *59,* 1262–1273.

Caldwell, C., and Pianta, R. C. "A Measure of Young Children's Problem and Competence Behaviors: The Early School Behavior Scale." *Journal of Psychoeducational Assessment,* 1991, *9,* 32–44.

Cassidy, J., and Marvin, R. S. "Attachment Organization in Three- and Four-Year-Olds: Coding Guidelines." Unpublished manuscript, University of Virginia, 1991.

Erickson, M. F., and Pianta, R. "New Lunchbox, Old Feelings: What Children Bring to School." *Early Education and Development,* 1989, *1,* 15–23.

Erickson, M. F., Sroufe, L. A., and Egeland, B. "The Relationship Between Quality of Attachment and Behavior Problems in Preschool in a High-Risk Sample." In I. Bretherton and E. Waters (eds.), *Growing Points of Attachment: Theory and Research.* Monographs of the Society for Research in Child Development, vol. 50, nos. 1–2 (serial no. 209). Chicago: University of Chicago Press, 1985.

Garmezy, N. "Stress-Resistant Children: The Search for Protective Factors." In J. E. Stevenson (ed.), *Aspects of Current Child Psychiatry Research.* Oxford, England: Pergamon Press, 1984.

Greenberg, M. T., Cicchetti, D., and Cummings, E. M. (eds.). *Attachment During the Preschool Years: Theory, Research, and Intervention.* Chicago: University of Chicago Press, 1990.

Greenberg, M. T., and Speltz, M. "Contributions of Attachment Theory to the Understanding of Conduct Problems During the Preschool Years." In J. Belsky and T. Nezworski (eds.), *Clinical Implications of Attachment.* Hillsdale, N.J.: Erlbaum, 1988.

Hightower, A. D., and others. "The Teacher-Child Rating Scale: A Brief Objective Measure of Children's Elementary School Problem Behaviors and Competencies." *School Psychology Review*, 1986, *15*, 393–409.

Hinde, R., and Stevenson-Hinde, J. "Interpersonal Relationships and Child Development." *Developmental Review*, 1987, *7*, 1–21.

Lewis, M., Feiring, C., McGuffog, C., and Jaskir, J. "Predicting Pathology in Six-Year-Olds from Early Social Relations." *Child Development*, 1984, *55*, 123–136.

Main, M., and Cassidy, J. "Categories of Response to Reunion with Parent at Age Six: Predictable from Infant Attachment and Stable Over a One-Month Period." *Developmental Psychology*, 1988, *24*, 415–426.

Minuchin, P., and Shapiro, E. "The School as a Context for Social Development." In E. M. Hetherington (ed.), *Handbook of Child Psychology*. Vol. 3: *Socialization and Personality Development*. New York: Wiley, 1983.

Nimetz, S. L. "Continuity from Mother-Child to Teacher-Child Relationships in Four-Year-Olds and the Prediction of Kindergarten Adjustment." Unpublished doctoral dissertation, Department of Education, University of Virginia, 1992.

Pederson, E., Faucher, T. A., and Eaton, W. W. "A New Perspective on the Effects of First-Grade Teachers on Children's Subsequent Adult Status." *Harvard Educational Review*, 1978, *48*, 1–31.

Pianta, R. C. "The Student-Teacher Relationship Scale." Unpublished manuscript, University of Virginia, 1990.

Pianta, R. C. "The Relationship Observation System." Unpublished manuscript, University of Virginia, 1991.

Pianta, R. C., and Nimetz, S. L. "Relationships Between Children and Teachers: Associations with Home and Classroom Behavior." *Journal of Applied Developmental Psychology*, 1991, *12*, 379–393.

Pianta, R. C., and Steinberg, M. "Relationships Between Children and Their Kindergarten Teachers." Paper presented at the biennial meeting of the Society for Research in Child Development, Seattle, Washington, April 1991.

Pianta, R. C., and others. "Early Predictors of Referrals for Special Services: Child-Based Measures vs. Mother-Child Interaction." *School Psychology Review*, 1990, *19*, 240–250.

Rutter, M. "Psychosocial Resilience and Protective Mechanisms." *American Journal of Orthopsychiatry*, 1987, *57*, 316–331.

Sameroff, A. J. "Principles of Development and Psychopathology." In A. J. Sameroff and R. N. Emde (eds.), *Relationship Disturbances in Early Childhood: A Developmental Approach*. New York: Basic Books, 1989.

Sroufe, L. A. "Infant-Caregiver Attachment and Patterns of Adaptation in Preschool: The Roots of Maladaptation and Competence." In M. Perlmutter (ed.), *Minnesota Symposia on Child Psychology*. Vol. 16. Hillsdale, N.J.: Erlbaum, 1983.

Sroufe, L. A. "Pathways to Adaptation and Maladaptation: Psychopathology as Developmental Deviation." In D. Cicchetti (ed.), *Emergence of a Discipline: Rochester Symposium on Developmental Psychopathology*. Hillsdale, N.J.: Erlbaum, 1989.

Sroufe, L. A., and Fleeson, J. "Attachment and the Construction of Relationships." In W. Hartup and Z. Rubin (eds.), *Relationships and Development*. Hillsdale, N.J.: Erlbaum, 1986.

Waters, E., and Deane, K. E. "The Attachment Q-Set." In I. Bretherton and E. Waters (eds.), *Growing Points of Attachment: Theory and Research*. Monographs of the Society for Research in Child Development, vol. 50, nos. 1–2 (serial no. 209). Chicago: University of Chicago Press, 1985.

Waters, E., and Sroufe, L. A. "Competence as an Organizational Construct." *Developmental Review*, 1983, *4*, 1–17.

Werner, E., and Smith, E. *Vulnerable but Invincible*. New York: Wiley, 1982.

ROBERT C. PIANTA is associate professor in the Curry Programs in School and Clinical Psychology, University of Virginia, Charlottesville. His research interests are in developmental psychopathology and the role of child-adult relationships in amelioration and exacerbation of risk.

MICHAEL STEINBERG is an advanced doctoral student in the Curry Programs in Clinical and School Psychology, University of Virginia.

Maltreated children's relationships with their teachers provide information about the coherence, role, and function of alternative or secondary attachments.

Maltreated Children's Reports of Relatedness to Their Teachers

Michael Lynch, Dante Cicchetti

Teachers form an important component of the milieu in which school-aged children develop. School teachers constitute a group of nonfamilial adults with whom children have extensive involvement for at least nine months of the year beginning at age five. Moreover, teachers may assume a variety of roles including caretaker, mentor, disciplinarian, and companion. The task of successfully negotiating relationships with teachers is important for children, and it may promote the attainment of competence in other school-related developmental domains.

Children's relationships with their teachers may be important for another reason as well. It is possible that teachers function as alternative or secondary attachment figures. The formation of attachment relationships with teachers may be especially helpful for children coming from stressful family environments characterized by maltreatment. It is possible that maltreated children's relationships with their teachers can act as protective factors against the negative developmental outcomes associated with maltreatment (Cicchetti, 1989, 1990; Cicchetti and Lynch, in press). Positive and secure relationships with teachers may begin to compensate for the negative relationship histories that maltreated children have with their parents by providing new information for these children's representational models of themselves and others. As a result, relationships with teachers may function as enduring compensatory factors for maltreated children (Cicchetti and Rizley, 1981). As a protective mechanism, these relationships can influence children's beliefs about themselves and others (Rutter, 1990).

We acknowledge the Spencer Foundation and the Spunk Fund, Inc., for their support of this work.

Research on relationships between children and nonparental adults can be aided by the perspective of developmental psychopathology (Cicchetti, 1984). With this point of view, research and theory on normative development informs our understanding of pathology, and investigations of pathology broaden our understanding of normal development. Thus, the study of maltreated children's relationships with their teachers provides an opportunity to understand the contributions that teachers make to children's development and adaptation. First, by examining teacher-child relationships in a group of children who are known to be at risk for relationship problems, it may be possible to identify precursors that influence the quality of children's relationships with teachers. This kind of information can increase our knowledge of the normative processes through which previous relationship histories influence subsequent relationships with novel partners. In addition, by investigating teacher-child relationships of maltreated children whose primary attachment figures provide little security and support, it may be possible to determine if children use their teachers as alternative or secondary attachment figures. With children who have experienced prominent and pervasive parent-child casualties, as is the case with maltreated children, it is possible to gain an understanding of how relationships to teachers influence children's adaptation to the immediate school environment as well as their more general developmental adaptation in ways that are not possible through the study of nonmaltreated children.

Of course, normal developmental theory can inform our understanding of potentially pathological processes involved in maltreated children's relationships with their teachers as well. Attachment theory, with its emphasis on the importance of representational models in predicting the behavior of actual and potential relationship partners, would suggest that maltreated children are likely to expect to have negative relationships with their teachers. In fact, how children's attachment systems influence the way in which they approach relationships with teachers has interesting implications for maltreated children's motivation for and performance in school. For maltreated children with insecure attachments, a general mistrust and wariness of others can result in the decreased ability to explore and master the environment. These deficiencies may leave maltreated children unprepared for school. Aber and his colleagues have found that maltreated children between four and eight years of age display less secure readiness to learn than do nonmaltreated children, a profile that is characterized by greater dependence on adults, lower effectance motivation, and lower cognitive maturity (Aber and Allen, 1987; Aber, Allen, Carlson, and Cicchetti, 1989). As a result, maltreated children are at risk for failure in school and poor resolution of many of the tasks associated with entering school (Cicchetti, 1989). These findings may indicate links among insecure attachment, decreased exploration, and low secure readiness to learn. The manner in which normal attachment processes exert influence on maltreated children's relationships with their teachers is one of the concerns of this chapter.

Internal Representational Models

Representational models may be one of the most important mechanisms through which the attachment system influences relationships with teachers. According to Bowlby's (1969, 1980) theory of attachment, early experiences with the caregiver are central in the formation of internal representational models of the self, others, and self-other relationships. These models allow children to form expectations about the availability and probable actions of others with complementary models of how worthy and competent the self is. Bretherton (1990) has suggested that representational models of the self and attachment figures may be hierarchically organized in terms of event schemas. Such a hierarchy would include low-level interactional schemas (for example, "When I get hurt, my mother comes to comfort and help me") and more general schemas (for example, "My mother is usually there for me when I need her"). At the top of the hierarchy would be overarching schemas such as "My mother is a loving person" and "I am loved and worthy of love." Attachment theory proposes that these organized mental representations are carried forward by the individual and used in subsequent interpersonal contexts.

Along these lines, Sroufe has demonstrated that the quality of preschool children's attachment histories with their primary caregivers influences their relationships with teachers (Sroufe, 1989; Sroufe and Fleeson, 1988). In the studies conducted by Sroufe and his colleagues, teacher contributions to these relationships were held constant by examining many children's relationships with the same teacher; as a result, it was possible to isolate the effects of children's attachment histories on teacher-child relationships. Coherent differences in teachers' behaviors were found to correlate with the children's attachment histories. For children with histories of secure attachment, teachers had higher expectations for compliance and age-appropriate behavior, but they needed to exert less control over these children. Children with avoidant attachment histories were treated with more discipline and control by teachers, and teachers had lower expectations of compliance from them. Avoidant-history children also were the only children who elicited anger responses from teachers. Children with resistant attachment histories also elicited higher levels of control from teachers. However, teachers also displayed more nurturance and tolerance toward these children. According to Sroufe, children's instantiated representational models of relationships play an important role in eliciting behavior from social partners such as teachers. In many ways, preschool children's relationships with their teachers may recapitulate their relationship histories with their caregivers, thus confirming internal representational models that are based on those relationship histories (Sroufe and Fleeson, 1988).

Self-organization plays a role in interpersonal development as well. From an organizational/relationship perspective, the self consists of an inner organization of feelings, meanings, expectations, and attitudes that emerges from an individual's relationship history (Sroufe, 1989). This self-organization has its origin in the self-regulation provided by the relationship with the primary caretaker. However, an individual's self-organization in turn influences the organization of ongoing and subsequent relationships.

Internal representational models may act as a mechanism of continuity in the transactions between self-organization and relationships with others. Observed continuities in the quality and pattern of interaction with different relationship figures can result from the increasingly internal organization of affects and beliefs that the individual possesses. Representational models of individual relationships contain information that is specific to those relationships. Expectations about the availability of the other person, how effective the self is likely to be in eliciting desired responses from the person, attitudes and commitment toward the relationship, and the affective tone of the relationship may all be incorporated into models of specific relationships. However, these specific models also may contribute information to more generalized models of relationships, the self, and others (Crittenden, 1990; Lynch and Cicchetti, 1991). It is possible that internal representational models of early attachment relationships begin to provide the individual with general information and expectations about how new social partners will act and react and how successful the self is likely to be in relation to those partners and the broader social context. Once again, though, the study of maltreated children may shed light on the processes involved in the formation and activation of generalized models. All children most likely use generalized representational models to generate expectations of others when confronted with novel adults. However, as the result of strongly aversive relationship experiences with their caregivers, maltreated children may be more likely than nonmaltreated and securely attached children to continue to relate to adults in accordance with their generalized models despite new and perhaps contrary experience with these adults. This continuity suggests that maltreated children's models may tend to be closed to new information. If a child's models are open, it may be easier to form specific representational models of new relationships. As a result, interpersonal relationships are likely to be influenced by a number of internal structures, including self-organization, specific representational models, and general representational models.

Interpersonal Relationships of Maltreated Children

It is well documented that maltreated children are more likely to experience and participate in maladaptive relationships than are nonmaltreated children. Heightened conflict, control, and punitive discipline techniques characterize the family environments of maltreated children (Trickett and Kuczynski, 1986; Wolfe, 1985). Furthermore, the emotional climate in maltreating families contributes to relational incompetence in children. For example, maltreating parents express little enjoyment in parenting and little affection for their children, they isolate themselves from the wider community, and they are less likely to encourage autonomy and independence in their children (Trickett, Aber, Carlson, and Cicchetti, 1991; Trickett and Sussman, 1988). Maltreated children's histories of experience in their families include feelings of insecurity, generalized fear, social isolation, and interpersonal loss (Carlson, Cicchetti, Barnett, and Braunwald, 1989b). As a result, maltreated children often approach relationships with a basic mistrust.

Attachment Relationships. One of the most consistent findings in the maltreatment literature is that maltreated children have a higher base rate of insecure attachments than do nonmaltreated children (Cicchetti and Barnett, 1991; Crittenden, 1988; Egeland and Sroufe, 1981; Schneider-Rosen, Braunwald, Carlson, and Cicchetti, 1985). Moreover, current research indicates the preponderance of disorganized/disoriented Type D attachments found in populations of young maltreated children. As many as 80 percent of maltreated infants may be classified as having a disorganized/disoriented attachment with their caregivers (Carlson, Cicchetti, Barnett, and Braunwald, 1989a, pp. 527–528), whereas less than 20 percent of demographically similar nonmaltreated children are observed to have Type D attachments, a behavioral pattern that is characterized in part by approach/avoidance conflicts and apprehension of the caregiver upon reunion (see Main and Solomon, 1990, for an in-depth treatment of Type D attachments). Similar findings have been reported by Lyons-Ruth, Repacholi, McLeod, and Silva (1991) and Crittenden (1988), who found that most maltreated children could be classified as having avoidant/ambivalent (A/C) patterns of attachment. Recently, in our laboratory, we have found substantial stability in D attachments across the ages of twelve, eighteen, and twenty-four months (Barnett, Ganiban, and Cicchetti, 1992). Approximately 60 percent of the infants who were classified as Type D at twelve months had the same classification at twenty-four months (Barnett, Ganiban, and Cicchetti, 1992), whereas over 90 percent of the infants classified as D at twenty-four months had previously received the D classification.

As maltreated children grow older, though, it appears less certain that they will develop one of these atypical patterns of attachment. In another investigation of the attachments of maltreated preschool children of different ages (Cicchetti and Barnett, 1991), thirty-month-old children who had been maltreated were significantly more likely to have atypical patterns of attachment (D or A/C) than were nonmaltreated children. However, even though approximately one-third of the thirty-six-month- and forty-eight-month-old maltreated children had either Type D or A/C attachments, this was not significantly greater than the proportion of nonmaltreated children who had such atypical attachment patterns. While it is conceivable that the attachment coding system for preschool children may utilize overly conservative criteria for detecting disorganization in the attachments of older children (Cassidy and Marvin, 1991), it also is possible that older children represent their maltreating attachment relationship in ways that are organized differently from the representations of younger children. Cognitive maturity may play a role in how children are able to represent maltreating relationships and themselves in such relationships, and how they are able to organize their attachment behavior strategies. Disorganization may be a characteristic feature of less differentiated and integrated mental representations and strategies. Severity and chronicity of abuse, as well as maltreatment history, probably also interact with cognitive maturity in determining the nature of mental representation. Perhaps the thirty-six-month- and forty-eight-month-old children described above received less severe or less chronic maltreatment than did the younger children. It is clear that many important questions regarding the manner in which relationship experiences and cognitive maturity interact as determinants of mental representation remain to be answered. Clearly, more longitudinal studies across these preschool ages must be conducted.

It is believed that the insecurity and disorganization found in many maltreated children's attachments are the result of the inconsistent care and fear that are common elements of maltreatment (Carlson, Cicchetti, Barnett, and Braunwald, 1989b; Main and Hesse, 1990). If maltreated children's representational models of self and others reflect insecurity and fear, and if these models are generalized to new relationships, then maltreated children may enter relationships with negative expectations that lead to the same type of approach/avoidance conflicts that are seen in their attachment relationships, resulting in maladaptive patterns of relating with their new partners.

Self-Development. A number of aspects of the self-development of maltreated children have implications for their interpersonal relationships as the result of inner self-organizations being brought forward into new social contexts. Although there are no deficits in maltreated infants' ability to recognize their rouge-marked selves in a mirror, they are more likely than nonmaltreated infants to display neutral or negative affect upon visual self-recognition (Schneider-Rosen and Cicchetti, 1984, 1991).

In addition, maltreated children talk less about themselves and produce less internal-state language than do comparison children (Cicchetti and Beeghly, 1987; Coster, Gersten, Beeghly, and Cicchetti, 1989). Maltreated children's negative feelings about themselves and their inability to talk about their own activities and feelings may pose one set of obstacles to their ability to engage in successful social interaction. In particular, maltreated children appear to be most resistant to talking about their negative internal states (Cicchetti and Beeghly, 1987). This finding is corroborated by reports that maltreated children may actually inhibit negative affect, especially in the context of the relationship with the caregiver (Crittenden and DiLalla, 1988; Lynch and Cicchetti, 1991). Maltreated children may adopt a strategy of suppressing their own negative feelings in order to avoid eliciting adverse responses from their caregivers (Cicchetti, 1991). While this approach may be adaptive in the context of a maltreating relationship, it can become maladaptive in other interpersonal contexts. For example, frustrated and upset children who are not willing or able to communicate what is bothering them can pose a serious challenge to a teacher trying to manage a classroom full of children.

Exposure to the school setting may have effects on maltreated children's sense of self that have implications for their relationships with others. Young maltreated children express an exaggerated sense of self-competence in comparison to nonmaltreated children (Vondra, Barnett, and Cicchetti, 1989). By the age of eight to nine years, though, maltreated children, compared to nonmaltreated, perceive themselves as less competent. Teachers' ratings of the children's competence indicate that these older children's perceptions are more accurate and in accord with their own ratings. Initially, young maltreated children's inflated sense of self may help them to gain feelings of competence in the midst of family relationships that are chaotic and uncontrollable. As maltreated children develop, though, and are forced to make social comparisons of themselves to others, they begin to make more negative (and accurate) self-appraisals. These negative appraisals likely are internalized in their self-representations. Their feelings of being less competent than others again may affect their ability to interact successfully with others.

Implications for the Role of Teacher-Child Relationships. From an organizational/relationship perspective, the difficulties documented in maltreated children's attachment relationships and self-development contribute to the formation of negative representational models. If maltreated children expect that others are unavailable and cannot be trusted, and that the self is incompetent, then it may be difficult for them as adolescents and adults to resolve developmental tasks surrounding issues of identity and intimacy and, in particular, to enter into nurturant relationships with their children. As a result, it is possible that maltreated children's models of self, others, and relationships function as a mechanism in the intergenerational transmission of maltreatment as well as in the development of more general maladaptation.

However, if maltreated children's representational models can be altered by new relationship experiences, then these altered models could provide a means for breaking the cycle of abuse and relational incompetence and maladaptation. An important finding in support of this hypothesis is that abused mothers who were able to break the abusive cycle with their children were more likely to have had a nonabusive, stable relationship with a mate and/or participated in therapy at some point in their lives (Egeland, Jacobvitz, and Sroufe, 1988). Of particular interest to understanding the importance of children's relationships with their teachers, though, is the finding that abusive mothers who broke the cycle of abuse were more likely to have received emotional support from a nonabusive adult during their childhood than were abused mothers who continued the cycle. It may be the case that a relationship with a supportive and nonabusive adult during childhood can provide maltreated children with corrective emotional experiences that alter or transform their models of self and others.

Teachers are a group of nonparental adults to which maltreated children have frequent exposure. Supportive experiences with teachers may begin to influence negative models of self and others and encourage maltreated children to become more engaged in school. The possibility of increased engagement in school is important because maltreated children are at risk for experiencing deficits in motivational orientation for achievement in school. To the extent that supportive relationships with teachers alter children's models of self and others, these relationships may encourage increased exploration and engagement in the environment. Furthermore, if maltreated children are able to experience success in school as the result of increased engagement, this experience could provide positive feedback to their models of self.

Issues that affect maltreated children's education have practical importance. Chronic poverty and the stress that it produces are associated with a higher incidence of maltreatment and typically extend across generations (Cicchetti and Lynch, in press). If maltreated children are able to engage in school and learning and are able to complete their education, then they may be able to escape from the economically deprived and stressful environments that contribute to maltreatment. Supportive relationships with teachers, then, may lead to multiple pathways that help maltreated children end the pattern of abuse and relational incompetence; one pathway proposes that relationships with teachers alter representational models of the self and others, while another (but not mutually exclusive) pathway hypothesizes that relationships with teachers increase children's engagement in school. Both of these pathways may enhance the successful resolution of current and subsequent developmental issues, thereby promoting competence and preventing maladaptation.

Construct of Relatedness

As children develop during the preschool and early school years, they gradually broaden their involvement in familial and extrafamilial relationship systems (Marvin and Stewart, 1990; Stevenson-Hinde, 1990). Participation in father-child systems, sibling systems, peer systems, and teacher-child systems, with their characteristic patterns of interaction, contribute to the development of play, collaboration, conflict resolution skills, and learning in ways that may not be possible solely within the mother-child relationship. In addition, if mothers are not present and children's attachment behavior systems are activated, they are likely to seek proximity to a person in the relationship system who can function as an alternative or secondary attachment figure, such as the father, an older sibling or peer, or a teacher (Ainsworth, 1989; Stewart and Marvin, 1984).

The construct of relatedness to others allows us to assess children's perceptions of the quality of these important relationship systems from the perspective of attachment and self-system theory. Wellborn and Connell (1987) have developed a self-report questionnaire that assesses that quality of children's feelings of relatedness to a variety of relationship figures. The need for relatedness, along with the need for competence and the need for autonomy, is one of three fundamental psychological needs in Connell's (1990) framework for self-system processes. The self-system is a set of appraisal processes with which the self evaluates the degree to which psychological needs are being met. The need for relatedness, with its roots in attachment theory, reflects the need to feel securely connected to the social surround and the need to experience oneself as worthy and capable of love (Connell, 1990). It seems possible that this type of information is incorporated into children's models of self and others. Appraisals of the degree to which these needs are being met would involve activation of the relevant representational models.

In theory, when individuals' feelings of relatedness to others are measured, they access an internal representational model of the specified relationship figure and of the self in relation to that figure. Information from both specific and general models of relationship figures may be evaluated (Crittenden, 1990; Lynch and Cicchetti, 1991). More specifically, information concerning factual knowledge about the relationship as well as affects connected to the relationship are recalled. By activating this storage base of knowledge and affect located in specific and general models of relationships, it is possible to assess an individual's feelings of relatedness to any specified relationship figure.

Investigation of Maltreated Children's Reports of Relatedness to Their Teachers

Recognizing the potential significance of maltreated children's relationships to their teachers, we conducted an investigation of maltreated and demographically matched nonmaltreated children's feelings of relatedness to their teachers. It was our prediction that maltreated children would make use of their teachers as alternative or secondary attachment figures, reflecting the need of their attachment systems to achieve feelings of security in some interpersonal context. However, based on attachment theory and guided by the relationship principles that were outlined above, it was our hypothesis that maltreated children would be overwhelmed by their prior relationship histories and their influence on mental representations and would report having less optimally secure and positive relationships with their teachers than would the non-maltreated children.

Sample. A total of 215 children participated in this investigation, including 115 children who had received services from the Monroe County Department of Social Services (New York) for issues related to maltreatment and 100 children from demographically matched families who had no documented history of maltreatment. The children in the study ranged in age from seven to thirteen years. There were 121 boys (59 maltreated, mean age of 9.2 years; and 62 nonmaltreated, mean age of 9.4 years) and 94 girls (54 maltreated, mean age of 9.5 years; and 40 nonmaltreated, mean age of 9.1 years) in the study.

The two groups of children came from families that were matched on multiple demographic variables, including welfare status, household income, number of adults in the home, number of children in the home, presence of an adult partner in the home, and marital status. All families were of low socioeconomic status. Table 5.1 presents a complete demographic breakdown of the sample. There were three demographic variables that indicated differences between maltreating and nonmaltreating families that were significant, two at the $p < .05$ level and one at the $p < .001$ level. First, while both groups of families had Hollingshead four-factor index scores that were extremely low, the scores for maltreating families were significantly lower than those for nonmaltreating families (maltreating Hollingshead = 19.3, SD = 7.1; nonmaltreating Hollingshead = 21.2, SD = 5.9). In addition, maltreating families on average had received welfare for a greater number of years than had nonmaltreating families, while nonmaltreating mothers had received slightly more education than maltreating mothers. None of the outcome variables in this study was associated with differences on these three demographic variables.

The families in the maltreatment group had all been assessed by public or private agencies to be in need of intervention services for issues connected to child maltreatment. Each family was documented as an official case of maltreatment under the criteria of New York State law following an investigation by the Department of Social Services. In each case, the mother was named as a perpetrator of maltreatment, although in 31 percent of the cases she was not the sole perpetrator. According to family case records, the maltreated children in our sample experienced the following different subtypes of maltreatment: physical abuse (36 percent), physical neglect (82 percent), emotional maltreatment (62 percent), sexual abuse (12 percent), and maltreatment associated with moral, legal, or educational issues (14 percent). Over two-thirds of the children experienced more than one form of maltreatment. The nonmaltreatment status of the comparison families was based on cross-checks with the state registry of maltreatment cases.

Procedure. All data were collected over a two-year period in the context of a summer camp conducted by the Mount Hope Family Center, a facility designed for treatment, prevention, research, and training in the area of family dysfunction and life-span developmental psychopathology. Children attended camp for one week during which time they

Table 5.1. Demographic Breakdown of Sample

	Maltreatment Group (N = 115)	Comparison Group (N = 100)	t-Test	χ^2
Currently on AFDC	85%	84%		ns
Number of years on AFDC	8.3	5.8	4.17[b]	
Household income	$12,900	$13,000	ns	
Number of adults in home	1.6	1.7	ns	
Number of children in home	3.0	2.7	ns	
Spouse/Partner in home				
Full time	35%	35%		ns
Half time	16%	27%		ns
None	49%	38%		ns
Marital status				
Single	24%	35%		ns
Married	20%	24%		ns
Divorced/Separated	38%	30%		ns
Cohabitating	13%	10%		ns
Highest grade completed by mother	10.9	11.3	2.11[a]	
Family Hollingshead score	19.3	21.2	2.02[a]	

Note: AFDC = Aid to Families with Dependent Children.
[a] $p < .05$
[b] $p < .001$

engaged in a variety of recreational activities under the close supervision of trained adult staff. Periodically throughout the week, children participated in a variety of research activities ranging from free-play sessions to semistructured interviews.

The relatedness scales were administered as part of an individual interview with each child in which the interviewer read the items to the child, the child indicated his or her response, and the interviewer recorded the response. Interviewers were blind to the children's maltreatment status. Items from the relatedness scales came from the Rochester Assessment Package for Schools (RAPS; Wellborn and Connell, 1987). The RAPS is a 261-item questionnaire that assesses children's feelings of competence, autonomy, and relatedness as they relate to feelings of engagement and disaffection in school. Using items from the RAPS, we asked the children in this study to answer questions about their feelings of relatedness to their teachers during the just-completed school year. In addition, children were asked to respond to another set of items regarding their feelings of relatedness to their mothers.

The relatedness scale has two distinct subscales: emotional quality and psychological proximity seeking. These two dimensions of relatedness are derived from a seventeen-item scale that produces a two-factor solution. Emotional quality is made up of eleven items that assess the overall affective tone of the relationship by asking about specific positive and negative emotions that children have when they are with the relationship partner. Children rated on a 4-point scale items such as "When I'm with my teacher, I feel happy." The specific emotions that were assessed included relaxed, ignored, happy, mad, bored, important, unhappy, scared, safe, and sad. For children's relationships with their mothers, they rated how much they felt "loved" when they were with their mothers. In addition, children were asked to rate the statement "I enjoy the time I spend with my teacher." Psychological proximity seeking includes six items that assess the degree to which children wish that they were psychologically closer to the relationship partner. Children rated on a 4-point scale items such as "I wish my teacher paid more attention to me" and "I wish my teacher knew me better."

The alpha reliabilities of internal consistency in previous normative samples range from .75 to .84 for emotional quality, and from .86 to .88 for psychological proximity seeking (Mellor-Crummey, 1989). Prior normative research using the relatedness scales indicates that the two dimensions of relatedness form patterns that are consistent with attachment and self-system theory (Connell and Wellborn, 1991; Lynch, 1990). In general, a report that the emotional quality of a relationship is positive with a specific relationship partner is associated with less of a need for greater psychological proximity to that partner. This positive correlation is consistent with attachment theory vis à vis felt security and the maintenance of physical proximity.

Results: Data Reduction and Scoring. Scores for each dimension of relatedness were created by calculating the mean score of the items in each factor. Therefore, each child received two scores: emotional quality with teacher and psychological proximity seeking with teacher. These scores were used in subsequent analyses. In addition, patterns of relatedness were determined by examining the configuration of individual children's scores on both dimensions of relatedness. These patterns were intended to capture the dynamic interaction between the two dimensions of relatedness.

Preliminary normative work in this area and our own work using high-risk urban samples have revealed five prototypical patterns of relatedness to mother derived from criterion cutoff scores on each dimension of relatedness (Lynch and Cicchetti, 1991). Initially, the selection of cutoff scores was guided by theoretical considerations of engaged versus disaffected patterns of action (see Connell, 1990) and by examinations of scatterplots from data collected on large normative samples. Subsequently, the structure of these patterns has been demonstrated in high-risk urban samples and supported by average linkage cluster analyses (Lynch and Cicchetti, 1991). These scores having been established for patterns of relatedness to mother, the same cutoff scores are used to determine patterns of relatedness to other relationship figures. Figure 5.1 shows the configurations of these patterns and their corresponding cutoff scores. Children who could not be assigned to one of the defined patterns of relatedness were labeled "unclassifiable." Historically in the attachment literature, children who could not be classified according to Ainsworth's original scheme (Ainsworth, Blehar, Waters, and Wall, 1978) invariably ended up being classified as insecure (Main and Solomon, 1990).

As indicated in Table 5.2, five different patterns of relatedness to teachers were found in our study sample: optimal, deprived, disengaged, confused, and average. Children with optimal patterns of relatedness to their teachers reported higher than average levels of positive emotion and lower than average amounts of psychological proximity seeking. These children felt positive and secure in their relationships, and they were satisfied with existing degrees of psychological closeness. Children with deprived patterns of relatedness to their teachers reported lower than average levels of emotional quality, but higher than average amounts of psychological proximity seeking. These children wanted to feel closer to their teachers, but their relationships were characterized by feelings of negativity and insecurity. Children with disengaged patterns of relatedness reported lower than average levels of emotional quality and lower than average amounts of psychological proximity seeking. These children had predominantly negative feelings about their teachers and did not want to be any closer to them. Children with confused patterns of relatedness reported high levels of emotional quality as well as extremely

Figure 5.1. Configurational Patterns of Relatedness to Teacher:
Emotional Quality and Psychological Proximity Seeking

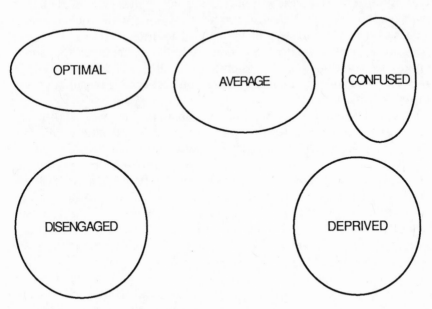

Note: Average: emotional quality > 3.0 and psychological proximity seeking > 2.0 and < 3.25; Confused: emotional quality > 3.0 and psychological proximity seeking > 3.25; Deprived: emotional quality ≤ 3.0 and psychological proximity seeking ≥ 3.0; Disengaged: emotional quality ≤ 3.0 and psychological proximity seeking ≤ 2.0; Optimal: emotional quality ≥ 3.5 and psychological proximity seeking ≤ 2.0.

Table 5.2. Percentage Distribution of Children with
Each Pattern of Relatedness to Teacher

Pattern	Maltreated		Nonmaltreated		χ^2
Optimal	.07	(8)	.19	(19)	6.17[a]
Deprived	.17	(19)	.17	(17)	0.00
Disengaged	.20	(23)	.21	(21)	0.02
Confused	.12	(14)	.08	(8)	0.94
Average	.05	(6)	.04	(4)	0.18
Unclassifiable	.40	(45)	.30	(31)	1.01

Note: Figures in parentheses are *N*'s.

[a] $p < .02$

high amounts of psychological proximity seeking. Despite having felt emotionally positive and secure in their relationships with their teachers, they felt that they needed much more psychological closeness. Finally, children with average patterns of relatedness to their teachers reported average levels of emotional quality and psychological proximity seeking.

Analyses. There was no correlation between emotional quality with teachers and psychological proximity seeking with teachers ($r = .00$). When the two dimensions of relatedness were examined individually, maltreated children reported more psychological proximity seeking with teachers than did nonmaltreated children (maltreated = 2.55, $SD = .90$; nonmaltreated = 2.27, $SD = .97$; $t = 2.17$, $p < .04$). Nonmaltreated children reported slightly more positive emotion with their teachers, but the difference was not significant (maltreated = 2.88, $SD = .66$; nonmaltreated = 3.04, $SD = .65$; $t = 1.77$, $p = .08$). There were no sex differences on either dimension of relatedness. However, univariate analyses indicated an effect of age on psychological proximity seeking with teachers ($F[6,196] = 2.32$, $p < .04$), with older children reporting that they wanted less psychological closeness with teachers than did younger children.

There was an overall effect of maltreatment status on children's patterns of relatedness with their teachers ($\chi^2[5] = 11.12$, $p < .05$). Specifically, maltreated children were less likely to report an optimal pattern of relatedness to their teachers than were nonmaltreated children ($\chi^2[1] = 6.17$, $p < .02$). However, it should be noted that close to 35 percent of the children had unclassifiable patterns of relatedness to their teachers using the cutoff criteria established for reports of relatedness to mothers. There were no group differences in the proportion of children who had unclassifiable patterns ($\chi^2[1] = 1.01$, $p > .20$).

When children's patterns of relatedness to their teachers were compared to their patterns of relatedness to their mothers, 38 percent of the children displayed concordance in their patterns of relatedness to both teacher and mother. This amount of concordance is significantly more than what would be expected by chance ($\chi^2[25] = 135.98$, $p < .0001$). Moreover, an analysis of variance indicated that a child's pattern of relatedness to mother had effects on both psychological proximity seeking with teachers ($F[4] = 17.54$, $p < .001$) and emotional quality with teachers ($F[4] = 7.06$, $p < .001$). Specifically, post hoc planned comparisons using the Tukey Studentized Range Test revealed that children with either a deprived or a confused pattern of relatedness to their mothers reported that they wished they were closer to their teachers significantly more than did children with other patterns of relatedness to mother. Similarly, children with optimal patterns of relatedness to their mothers reported the highest levels of positive affect and security with teachers, while children with deprived patterns reported the lowest levels. Table 5.3 shows the mean scores for psychological proximity seeking with teacher and emotional quality with teacher for each pattern of relatedness to mother.

Discussion

The investigation reported above has its limitations. It is important to point out that we do not claim that patterns of relatedness are patterns of attachment. Although the construct of relatedness may assess attachment-related issues, the necessary studies linking self-reported patterns of relatedness to attachment behaviors have not been carried out yet. Until these studies, as well as longitudinal studies linking attachment with relatedness, have been conducted, it is difficult to make strong claims about the predicted continuity between early attachment history and subsequent patterns of relatedness based on mental representations and previous relationship experience. Moreover, the fact that 35 percent of the children in this study had patterns of relatedness to their teachers that were unclassifiable using the cutoff scores established for relationships with mothers suggests that there is a need to develop separate cutoff scores for relationships with nonparental adults.

In addition, contrary to findings on children's reports of relatedness to other relationship figures such as their mothers, best friends, and

Table 5.3. Mean Scores for Psychological Proximity Seeking and Emotional Equality with Teachers for Different Patterns of Relatedness to Mother

Pattern of Relatedness to Mother	Psychological Proximity Seeking to Teacher	Emotional Equality with Teacher
Deprived	3.05[b,c,d]	2.50[a,d]
Confused	3.00[e,f,g]	3.05[a]
Average	2.35[b,e]	2.94
Disengaged	1.85[c,f]	2.63
Optimal	1.80[d,g]	3.27[d]

[a] Difference between deprived and confused, $p < .05$.

[b] Difference between deprived and average, $p < .05$.

[c] Difference between deprived and disengaged, $p < .05$.

[d] Difference between deprived and optimal, $p < .05$.

[e] Difference between confused and average, $p < .05$.

[f] Difference between confused and disengaged, $p < 05$.

[g] Difference between confused and optimal, $p < .05$.

classmates (Lynch and Cicchetti, 1991), there was no coherent association between the two dimensions of relatedness for children's relationships with their teachers. It may be the case that children's relationships with their teachers are not intimate enough to activate self-system appraisals of how well needs for relatedness are being met. The lack of a clear association between psychological proximity seeking with teachers and emotional quality with teachers also may indicate that children's relationships with their teachers are not mentally represented with an internal organization that is consistent with the needs of the attachment behavior system. Perhaps teachers assume too many other roles that make it difficult for children to see and make use of them as alternative attachment figures as well. Alternatively, it may be that only children in extreme psychological need regularly look to their teachers to fill attachment-related roles, for example, children who are emotionally neglected or otherwise maltreated by their primary caregivers.

However, when individual children's patterns of relatedness were examined, the findings were consistent with previous research on maltreated children's maladaptive relationship histories with social partners. The finding that maltreated children were less likely to have optimal patterns of relatedness than were nonmaltreated children may be a sign that maltreated children are carrying representational models based on their interactional histories with their caregivers forward with them into new relationship contexts. A total of 38 percent of the children in this study had patterns of relatedness to their teachers that were concordant with their patterns of relatedness to their mothers.

Additional evidence that representational models of the relationship with mother might influence models of other relationships is the finding that children's patterns of relatedness to their mothers are related to both dimensions of relatedness to teachers. There appears to be a link at the level of mental representation between the manner in which children internally organize their relationships with their mothers and their reports of relatedness to teachers. Children with optimal models of their relationships with their mothers may be more able to experience positive affect and security with other adults such as teachers than are children with less optimal models. On the other hand, children who have less optimal models may need to look outside their relationships with their mothers for psychological closeness and support. It may be the case that these children wish that they were closer to their teachers, more so than other children, in order to compensate for not feeling close to their mothers. It makes sense, then, that maltreated children, who tend to experience less secure relationships with their mothers, would express a greater desire for psychological closeness to another adult than expressed by nonmaltreated children, even though they currently may be less able to feel positive affect about that adult. Deprived patterns of relatedness to mother may be the most disruptive for forming productive relationships with teachers. Children with deprived patterns reported the highest levels of wanting to be closer to their teachers, while also reporting the lowest levels of positive affect and security with teachers, a pattern of scores with teachers that to some extent recapitulates their relationships with their mothers.

The ability to establish a positive relationship with a teacher may be an important step in promoting resilient outcomes for some maltreated children. An emotionally supportive relationship with a nonabusive adult has been identified as a potentially protective factor in breaking the cycle of maltreatment in abused mothers (Egeland, Jacobvitz, and Sroufe, 1988). Furthermore, children who do well by competently resolving stage-salient tasks despite developmental adversity repeatedly have been found to be able to connect with at least one important person (Masten, Best, and Garmezy, 1990). If maltreated children are less able to engage in optimal relationships with their teachers, then they may be cutting themselves off from possible sources of corrective emotional experiences that could alter their models of self and others. The fact that we found only moderate concordance between patterns of relatedness to mothers and to teachers suggests, though, that maltreated children do not *necessarily* organize their models of relationships with teachers in accordance with their representations of their relationships with their mothers. On the contrary, perhaps some maltreated children, rather than relying solely on closed generalized models, are able to maintain open representational models that differentiate new specific models. The possibility still exists, then, for maltreated children to engage in more positive patterns of relating to teachers than they do with their mothers. In order to capitalize on this possibility, it may be important to include knowledge about developmental theory, attachment relationships, and child maltreatment in the training of teachers (Cicchetti, Toth, and Hennessy, 1989). This increased knowledge may help teachers to respond more appropriately to the needs of maltreated children, thus increasing the chance for a more productive teacher-child relationship. If teachers understand their potential role as an alternative or secondary attachment figure, then they may be able to foster the building of trust that will help maltreated children negotiate relationships with other partners.

Finally, we suggested that one additional pathway through which maltreated children might break the cycle of abuse was increased engagement in school. The challenge for maltreated children to succeed in school is real, though. Maltreated children's representational models reflect insecure attachment histories and, as a result, their attachment behavior systems are continually activated, reflecting a preoccupation with needs for safety, love, and acceptance. Therefore, it is unlikely that maltreated children's exploratory behavior systems are able to be activated fully to meet needs for feelings of effectance. In fact, maltreated children demonstrate lower levels of effectance motivation than do nonmaltreated children (Aber, Allen, Carlson, and Cicchetti, 1989). Moreover, specific parenting styles in maltreating families may contribute to motivational deficits in children. Trickett and Susman (1988) have demonstrated that maltreating parents have higher achievement orientations than do nonmaltreating parents, as well as more controlling disciplinary styles. The combination of high performance demands and a controlling environment has been linked to extrinsic motivational orientations (Koestner, Ryan, Bernieri, and Holt, 1984), which are considered maladaptive for children's classroom performance (Ryan, Connell, and Deci, 1985). On the other hand, children with secure attachments may have more time to engage their exploratory behavior systems and satisfy needs for effectance and mastery.

A supportive relationship with a teacher may be a factor that helps maltreated children become engaged in school. Normative data have shown a positive correlation between emotional quality with teachers and engagement in school ($r = .23$, $p < .001$; see Connell and Wellborn, 1991, p. 63). If we apply this finding to maltreated children, then we might predict that emotionally supportive relationships with teachers, in addition to influencing models of self and others, might help maltreated children become more engaged in school. Although there is evidence to suggest that, on average, maltreated children perform poorly in school (Erickson, Egeland, and Pianta, 1989; Vondra, Barnett, and Cicchetti, 1989), increased engagement through positive relationships with teachers is one possible mechanism to explain why some maltreated children perform adequately in school. Data that we are collecting in the schools, in combination with concurrent relatedness data, will allow us to test this hypothesis.

Future Directions and Recommendations

It is likely that there are a number of relationships with partners other than an individual's primary caregiver that can serve attachment-related functions (Ainsworth, 1989; Marvin and Stewart, 1990); however, an understanding of the role and organization of these alternative attachments poses some significant challenges. Researchers interested in investigating children's relationships with nonparental adults and their broadening involvement in relationship systems other than those with their primary caregivers need to consider several related theoretical and methodological issues. We have attempted to address these issues in our investigation of children's reports of relatedness to their teachers.

First, the stage salience of developmental tasks and issues as they impact the attachment system must be taken into account. As Bowlby

(1969) described, one of the primary tasks of development beginning in the preschool years is to form a "goal-corrected partnership" with one's attachment figures (Cicchetti, Cummings, Greenberg, and Marvin, 1990; Marvin, 1977). This increasingly internalized partnership reflects a child's ability to share goals, plans, and internal states with his or her attachment figures, and not just physical proximity.

Second, attachments become increasingly representational in nature and operation as children grow older (Bretherton, 1985; Crittenden and Ainsworth, 1989). The primary caregiver no longer needs to be physically present for the child to feel secure. Internal representations of the attachment figure are called upon when the child feels distress. This becomes possible because similar relationship events have been encoded into episodic memory where they are organized into prototypical memories (Stern, 1989). These prototypes are representations of general emotions and cognitions, events, and behavioral patterns located in the semantic, episodic, and procedural memory systems, respectively (Crittenden, 1990; Tulving, 1985, 1989).

Research on the formation and organization of representational models provides an example of a normative domain of inquiry that is aided by the study of an atypical population. In particular, our investigations of maltreated children's relationships and self-system processes are offering evidence that cognitive maturation plays a role in the structural organization of representational models of the self and others. For example, Cicchetti and Barnett (1991) have found that disorganized attachments appear to be less common in preschool-age maltreated children than they are in maltreated infants. Older children may be able to organize better their behavioral strategies as the result of more coherent mental representations. However, as Lynch and Cicchetti (1991) have discussed in their investigations of maltreated children's patterns of relatedness to their mothers, for some children representational disorganization or confusion may continue through the early school years. It is noteworthy that children who had such confused patterns of relatedness to their mothers were younger than children with other patterns, again suggesting an association between inner organization and cognitive maturation. Cognitive maturation may even influence the organization of self-representations, as the shift in maltreated children's appraisals of their own competence around the third or fourth grade suggests (Vondra, Barnett, and Cicchetti, 1989). This growing body of evidence indicating the importance of cognitive maturation in the organization of mental representational models is largely the result of the study of children whose representations of themselves and others are pushed to distorted extremes by the experience of maltreatment.

A final point that is important for researchers to consider is that measurement becomes an issue in primary and alternative attachments beyond infancy. Classification schemes based solely on behavior probably are inappropriate for older children. Rather, multimethod indices of attachment in multiple contexts, the assessment of internal representational models, and the use of continua ratings of felt security are more appropriate ways of assessing the quality of attachment in older children (Cicchetti, Cummings, Greenberg, and Marvin, 1990). We believe that the construct of relatedness provides researchers with one method of assessing attachment-related issues in older children.

Do children's relationships with their teachers function as alternative attachments, and, more specifically, can maltreated children make use of them as such? The question of whether or not teachers can function as alternative attachment figures was not answered definitively in this study, although it did not appear that the children in our sample had mentally represented their relationships to their teachers in an organized manner that was consistent with attachment theory. However, if maltreated children could use their relationships with their teachers as alternative or secondary attachments, then these relationships could act as significant protective factors against wide-ranging maladaptation in maltreated children. Unfortunately, a number of factors seem to undermine the ability of maltreated children to form attachments with their teachers.

For a variety of reasons, maltreated children often have little opportunity to establish long-term, intimate relationships with their teachers. The families in our sample are very mobile, and the children may change schools several times in one year. This kind of instability makes it difficult to form any kind of meaningful relationship with a teacher. Rather, the repeated moves may add to the experience of loss and unavailability of significant adults that becomes incorporated into maltreated children's representational models. Moreover, the way that schooling is structured can make it difficult for children with self- and interpersonal deficits to form intimate relationships with teachers. During the elementary school years, children change teachers every year, and once they advance to secondary school, they no longer have one primary teacher with whom to relate. While children with healthier representational models likely are able to form important relationships with teachers, children whose representational models of others are organized around fear and mistrust may have understandable difficulty in getting close to a novel adult during the course of one school year.

The fact that maltreated children bring negative models of relationships with them to the context of teacher-child relationships further hinders their ability to take advantage of potentially supportive relationships with teachers. Initially, children's specific and general models of self and others remain more or less open to new input and subsequent readjustment (Crittenden and Ainsworth, 1989). Early on, as children experience additional interactions with their relationship partners, they are able to readily assimilate these experiences into their existing models or accommodate their models to new information if necessary. However, with increasing verbal abilities and cognitive development, children's representational models may become more closed to new inputs by the school-age years (Crittenden and Ainsworth, 1989). Conceptual processes replace actual episodes of experience in the formulation and integration of representational models. It may not be until adolescence, when children attain formal operations, that a rethinking of previous experiences is likely to occur. Closed models may be particularly detrimental to children who have experienced insecure attachments and/or maltreatment. Parents' explanations that their harsh behavior is for their children's own good become organizing themes for children's models of themselves and others. As a result, these children's representations of themselves and others may not be open to alternative and potentially positive experiences with others, including teachers. Instead, they base their interactions on negative expectations, leading to less competent dealings with others. Repeated experiences of incompetent interactions with others serve to confirm their negative representational models, making it even less likely that they will be open to positive interpersonal experiences in the future.

Clearly there are many factors that make it difficult for maltreated children to negotiate successful relationships with their teachers and to use them to promote increased interpersonal competence. However, research on child maltreatment has many practical implications for policies connected to the training of teachers and the structuring of classrooms that can increase the chances that the teacher-child relationship will promote adaptation. Crittenden (1989) suggests that maltreated children have special needs that leave them unprepared for school. As the result of unpredictable and uncontrollable home environments, maltreated children have very basic needs to experience predictability and socially appropriate control in their environments. For teachers to create this type of environment requires much more individualized attention than is available in most classrooms (Crittenden, 1989). Additionally, a fostering of the development of language and communication skills in maltreated children may increase their ability to relate effectively with others. Finally, teachers who can offer consistent affective experiences will help maltreated children to develop trust in others. Toward this end, it is important for teachers not to mix discipline and caring. Maltreated children have difficulty integrating the mixed message of firmness and caring; therefore, discipline should be carried out with neutral affect (Crittenden, 1989). Maltreated children can then learn to trust signs of positive regard from others. However, in order for improvements in children's interpersonal competence to generalize beyond the classroom, all of these steps need to be taken with an approach that will integrate parents and families into the therapeutic process. Without supportive counseling and education, maltreating parents may not be ready for, or approve of, changes in their children's ability to communicate their own needs and desires or their attempts to achieve goal-corrected partnerships (Cicchetti, Toth, and Bush, 1988).

While the findings presented in this paper are limited in their ability to suggest policy changes in schools, it is clear that our current body of knowledge about the consequences of maltreatment for children's development demands that we no longer tolerate a lack of action on behalf of maltreated children in the schools. Maltreated children have special needs beyond their linguistic and cognitive impairments. They have emotional difficulties that must be addressed by both teachers and school psychologists (Cicchetti, 1990). In fact, schools increasingly need to become concerned with what happens to children outside of the classroom. More attention needs to be paid to the emotional health of children and to the role of family systems. Intense training of teachers and long-term efforts by schools are required to take advantage of teacher-child relationships; however, relationships to teachers are a potentially protective factor available to all children, and they can begin to counteract the consequences of maltreatment and alter children's expectations about themselves, others, and relationships (Erickson, Egeland, and Pianta, 1989). Attempts by researchers to understand better the role and function of nonparental relationships, such as those with teachers, only can help to increase the amount of aid and services that are made available to maltreated children.

References

Aber, J. L., and Allen, J. "The Effects of Maltreatment on Young Children's Socioemotional Development: An Attachment Theory Perspective." *Developmental Psychology,* 1987, 23 (3), 406–414.

Aber, J. L., Allen, J., Carlson, V., and Cicchetti, D. "The Effects of Maltreatment on Development During Early Childhood: Recent Studies and Their Theoretical, Clinical, and Policy Implications." In D. Cicchetti and V. Carlson (eds.), *Child Maltreatment: Theory and Research on the Causes and Consequences of Child Abuse and Neglect.* New York: Cambridge University Press, 1989.

Ainsworth, M.D.S. "Attachments Beyond Infancy." *American Psychologist,* 1989, 44 (4), 709–716.

Ainsworth, M.D.S., Blehar, M. C., Waters, E., and Wall, S. *Patterns of Attachment: A Psychological Study of the Strange Situation.* Hillsdale, N.J.: Erlbaum, 1978.

Barnett, D., Ganiban, J., and Cicchetti, D. "Temperament and Behavior of Youngsters with Disorganized Attachments: A Longitudinal Study." Paper presented at the International Conference on Infant Studies, Miami, Florida, April 1992.

Bowlby, J. *Attachment and Loss.* Vol. 1: *Attachment.* New York: Basic Books, 1969.

Bowlby, J. *Attachment and Loss.* Vol. 3: *Loss, Sadness, and Depression.* New York: Basic Books, 1980.

Bretherton, I. "Attachment Theory: Retrospect and Prospect." In I. Bretherton and E. Waters (eds.), *Growing Points of Attachment: Theory and Research.* Monographs of the Society for

Research in Child Development, vol. 50, nos. 1–2 (serial no. 209). Chicago: University of Chicago Press, 1985.

Bretherton, I. "Open Communication and Internal Working Models: Their Role in the Development of Attachment Relationships." In R. A. Thompson (ed.), *Socioemotional Development*. Nebraska Symposia on Motivation, vol. 36. Lincoln: University of Nebraska Press, 1990.

Carlson, V., Cicchetti, D., Barnett, D., and Braunwald, K. "Disorganized/Disoriented Attachment Relationships in Maltreated Infants." *Developmental Psychology*, 1989a, 25 (4), 525–531.

Carlson, V., Cicchetti, D., Barnett, D., and Braunwald, K. "Finding Order in Disorganization: Lessons from Research on Maltreated Infants' Attachments to Their Caregivers." In D. Cicchetti and V. Carlson (eds.), *Child Maltreatment: Theory and Research on the Causes and Consequences of Child Abuse and Neglect*. New York: Cambridge University Press, 1989b.

Cassidy, J., and Marvin, R. S. "Attachment Organization in Three- and Four-Year Olds: Coding Guidelines." Unpublished manuscript, University of Virginia, 1991.

Cicchetti, D. "The Emergence of Developmental Psychopathology." *Child Development*, 1984, 55 (1), 1–7.

Cicchetti, D. "How Research on Child Maltreatment Has Informed the Study of Child Development: Perspectives from Developmental Psychopathology." In D. Cicchetti and V. Carlson (eds.), *Child Maltreatment: Theory and Research on the Causes and Consequences of Child Abuse and Neglect*. New York: Cambridge University Press, 1989.

Cicchetti, D. "The Organization and Coherence of Socioemotional, Cognitive, and Representational Development: Illustrations Through a Developmental Psychopathology Perspective on Down Syndrome and Child Maltreatment." In R. A. Thompson (ed.), *Socioemotional Development*. Nebraska Symposia on Motivation, vol. 36. Lincoln: University of Nebraska Press, 1990.

Cicchetti, D. "Fractures in the Crystal: Developmental Psychopathology and the Emergence of Self." *Developmental Review*, 1991, 11, 1–21.

Cicchetti, D., and Barnett, D. "Attachment Organization in Maltreated Preschoolers." *Development and Psychopathology*, 1991, 3 (4), 397–411.

Cicchetti, D., and Beeghly, M. "Symbolic Development in Maltreated Youngsters: An Organizational Perspective." In D. Cicchetti and M. Beeghly (eds.), *Symbolic Development in Atypical Children*. New Directions for Child Development, no. 36. San Francisco: Jossey-Bass, 1987.

Cicchetti, D., Cummings, E. M., Greenberg, M., and Marvin, R. "An Organizational Perspective on Attachment Theory Beyond Infancy: Implications for Theory, Measurement, and Research." In M. T. Greenberg, D. Cicchetti, and E. M. Cummings (eds.), *Attachment During the Preschool Years: Theory, Research, and Intervention*. Chicago: University of Chicago Press, 1990.

Cicchetti, D., and Lynch, M. "Toward an Ecological/Transactional Model of Community Violence and Child Maltreatment: Consequences for Children's Development." *Psychiatry*, in press.

Cicchetti, D., and Rizley, R. "Developmental Perspectives on the Etiology, Intergenerational Transmission, and Sequelae of Child Maltreatment." In R. Rizley and D. Cicchetti (eds.), *Developmental Perspectives on Child Maltreatment*. New Directions for Child Development, no. 11. San Francisco: Jossey-Bass, 1981.

Cicchetti, D., Toth, S., and Bush, B. "Developmental Psychopathology and Incompetence in Childhood: Suggestions for Intervention." In B. Lahey and A. Kazdin (eds.), *Advances in Clinical Child Psychology*. New York: Plenum, 1988.

Cicchetti, D., Toth, S., and Hennessy, K. "Research on the Consequences of Child Maltreatment and Its Applications to Educational Settings." *Topics in Early Childhood Education*, 1989, 9 (2), 33–55.

Connell, J. P. "Context, Self, and Action: A Motivational Analysis of Self-System Processes Across the Life-Span." In D. Cicchetti and M. Beeghly (eds.), *The Self in Transition: Infancy to Childhood*. Chicago: University of Chicago Press, 1990.

Connell, J. P., and Wellborn, J. G. "Competence, Autonomy and Relatedness: A Motivational Analysis of Self-System Processes." In M. Gunnar and L. A. Sroufe (eds.), *Minnesota Symposia on Child Psychology*. Vol. 22. Hillsdale, N.J.: Erlbaum, 1991.

Coster, W. J., Gersten, M. S., Beeghly, M., and Cicchetti, D. "Communicative Functioning in Maltreated Toddlers." *Developmental Psychology*, 1989, 25 (6), 1020–1029.

Crittenden, P. M. "Relationships at Risk." In J. Belsky and T. N. Nezworski (eds.), *Clinical Implications of Attachment*. Hillsdale, N.J.: Erlbaum, 1988.

Crittenden, P. M. "Teaching Maltreated Children in the Preschool." *Topics in Early Childhood Education*, 1989, 9 (2), 16–32.

Crittenden, P. M. "Internal Representational Models of Attachment Relationships." *Infant Mental Health Journal*, 1990, 11 (3), 259–277.

Crittenden, P. M., and Ainsworth, M.D.S. "Attachment and Child Abuse." In D. Cicchetti and V. Carlson (eds.), *Child Maltreatment: Theory and Research on the Causes and Consequences of Child Abuse and Neglect*. New York: Cambridge University Press, 1989.

Crittenden, P. M., and DiLalla, D. L. "Compulsive Compliance: The Development of an Inhibitory Coping Strategy in Infancy." *Journal of Abnormal Child Psychology*, 1988, 16 (5), 585–599.

Egeland, B., Jacobvitz, D., and Sroufe, L. A. "Breaking the Cycle of Abuse." *Child Development*, 1988, 59 (4), 1080–1088.

Egeland, B., and Sroufe, L. A. "Developmental Sequelae of Maltreatment in Infancy." In R. Rizley and D. Cicchetti (eds.), *Developmental Perspectives on Child Maltreatment*. New Directions for Child Development, no. 11. San Francisco: Jossey-Bass, 1981.

Erickson, M. F., Egeland, B., and Pianta, R. "The Effects of Maltreatment on the Development of Young Children." In D. Cicchetti and V. Carlson (eds.), *Child Maltreatment: Theory and Research on the Causes and Consequences of Child Abuse and Neglect*. New York: Cambridge University Press, 1989.

Koestner, R., Ryan, R. M., Bernieri, F., and Holt, K. "Setting Limits on Children's Behavior: The Differential Effects of Controlling Versus Informational Styles on Intrinsic Motivation and Creativity." *Journal of Personality*, 1984, 52 (3), 233–248.

Lynch, M. "Children's Relatedness to Peers: Attachment Beyond Infancy and Its Organization Across Relationships." Unpublished master's thesis, Department of Psychology, University of Rochester, 1990.

Lynch, M., and Cicchetti, D. "Patterns of Relatedness in Maltreated and Nonmaltreated Children: Connections Among Multiple Representational Models." *Development and Psychopathology*, 1991, 3 (2), 207–226.

Lyons-Ruth, K., Repacholi, B., McLeod, S., and Silva, E. "Disorganized Attachment Behavior in Infancy: Short-Term Stability, Maternal and Infant Correlates." *Development and Psychopathology*, 1991, 3 (4), 377–396.

Main, M., and Hesse, E. "Parents' Unresolved Traumatic Experiences Are Related to Infant Disorganized Attachment Status: Is Frightened and/or Frightening Parental Behavior the Linking Mechanism?" In M. T. Greenberg, D. Cicchetti, and E. M. Cummings (eds.), *Attachment During the Preschool Years: Theory, Research, and Intervention*. Chicago: University of Chicago Press, 1990.

Main, M., and Solomon, J. "Procedures for Identifying Infants as Disorganized/Disoriented During the Ainsworth Strange Situation." In M. T. Greenberg, D. Cicchetti, and E. M. Cummings (eds.), *Attachment During the Preschool Years: Theory, Research, and Intervention*. Chicago: University of Chicago Press, 1990.

Marvin, R. S. "An Ethological-Cognitive Model for the Attenuation of Mother-Child Attachment Behavior." In T. M. Alloway, L. Krames, and P. Piner (eds.), *Advances in the Study of Communication and Affect*. Vol. 3: *The Development of Social Attachments*. New York: Plenum, 1977.

Marvin, R. S., and Stewart, R. B. "A Family Systems Framework for the Study of Attachment." In M. T. Greenberg, D. Cicchetti, and E. M. Cummings (eds.), *Attachment During the*

Preschool Years: Theory, Research, and Intervention. Chicago: University of Chicago Press, 1990.

Masten, A. S., Best, K. M., and Garmezy, N. "Resilience and Development: Contributions from the Study of Children Who Overcome Adversity." *Development and Psychopathology,* 1990, 2 (4), 425–444.

Mellor-Crummey, C. "Social Coping in Children." Unpublished doctoral dissertation, Department of Psychology, University of Rochester, 1989.

Rutter, M. "Psychosocial Resilience and Protective Mechanisms." In J. Rolf, A. Masten, D. Cicchetti, K. Neuchterlein, and S. Weintraub (eds.), *Risk and Protective Factors in the Development of Psychopathology.* New York: Cambridge University Press, 1990.

Ryan, R. M., Connell, J. P., and Deci, E. L. "A Motivational Analysis of Self-Determination and Self-Regulation in Education." In C. Ames and P. E. Ames (eds.), *Research on Motivation in Education: The Classroom Milieu.* San Diego, Calif.: Academic Press, 1985.

Schneider-Rosen, K., Braunwald, K., Carlson, V., and Cicchetti, D. "Current Perspectives in Attachment Theory: Illustration from the Study of Maltreated Infants." In I. Bretherton and E. Waters (eds.), *Growing Points of Attachment: Theory and Research.* Monographs of the Society for Research in Child Development, vol. 50, nos. 1–2 (serial no. 209). Chicago: University of Chicago Press, 1985.

Schneider-Rosen, K., and Cicchetti, D. "The Relationship Between Affect and Cognition in Maltreated Infants: Quality of Attachment and the Development of Visual Self-Recognition." *Child Development,* 1984, 55 (2), 648–658.

Schneider-Rosen, K., and Cicchetti, D. "Early Self-Knowledge and Emotional Development: Visual Self-Recognition and Affective Reactions to Mirror Self-Images in Maltreated and Non-Maltreated Toddlers." *Developmental Psychology,* 1991, 27 (3), 471–478.

Sroufe, L. A. "Relationships, Self, and Individual Adaptation." In A. J. Sameroff and R. N. Emde (eds.), *Relationship Disturbances in Early Childhood: A Developmental Approach.* New York: Basic Books, 1989.

Sroufe, L. A., and Fleeson, J. "The Coherence of Family Relationships." In R. A. Hinde and J. Stevenson-Hinde (eds.), *Relationships Within Families: Mutual Influences.* Oxford, England: Clarendon Press, 1988.

Stern, D. N. "The Representation of Relational Patterns: Developmental Considerations." In A. J. Sameroff and R. N. Emde (eds.), *Relationship Disturbances in Early Childhood: A Developmental Approach.* New York: Basic Books, 1989.

Stevenson-Hinde, J. "Attachment Within Family Systems: An Overview." *Infant Mental Health Journal,* 1990, 11 (3), 218–227.

Stewart, R., and Marvin, R. S. "Sibling Relations: The Role of Conceptual Perspective-Taking in the Ontogeny of Sibling Caregiving." *Child Development,* 1984, 55 (4), 1322–1332.

Trickett, P., Aber, J. L., Carlson, V., and Cicchetti, D. "Relationship of Socioeconomic Status to the Etiology and Developmental Sequelae of Physical Child Abuse." *Developmental Psychology,* 1991, 27 (1), 148–158.

Trickett, P., and Kuczynski, L. "Children's Behaviors and Parental Discipline in Abusive and Nonabusive Families." *Developmental Psychology,* 1986, 22 (1), 115–123.

Trickett, P., and Sussman, E. J. "Parental Perceptions of Childrearing Practices in Physically Abusive and Nonabusive Families." *Developmental Psychology,* 1988, 24 (2), 270–276.

Tulving, E. "How Many Memory Systems Are There?" *American Psychologist,* 1985, 40 (4), 385–398.

Tulving, E. "Remembering and Knowing the Past." *American Scientist,* 1989, 77 (3), 361–367.

Vondra, J., Barnett, D., and Cicchetti, D. "Perceived and Actual Competence Among Maltreated and Comparison School Children." *Development and Psychopathology,* 1989, 1 (3), 237–256.

Wellborn, J. G., and Connell, J. P. "Manual for the Rochester Assessment Package for Schools." Unpublished manuscript, University of Rochester, 1987.

Wolfe, D. A. "Child Abusive Parents: An Empirical Review and Analysis." *Psychological Bulletin,* 1985, 97 (3), 467–482.

MICHAEL LYNCH is an advanced doctoral student in developmental psychology at the University of Rochester. Since 1988, he has been the coordinator of the summer camp and after-school programs at Mount Hope Family Center in Rochester, New York. His research interests include child maltreatment, attachment relationships, peer relationships, and mental representation from the perspective of developmental psychopathology.

DANTE CICCHETTI is director of Mount Hope Family Center, professor of psychology and psychiatry at the University of Rochester, and editor of Development and Psychopathology. His primary theoretical and research interests are in the areas of developmental psychopathology and developmental neuroscience.

Children's relationships provide a useful lens through which to view the role of continuity and context in children's development.

The Role of Continuity and Context in Children's Relationships with Nonparental Adults

Susan Kontos

Because the majority of children from infancy through age five and virtually all children from age five through eighteen spend significant amounts of time under the supervision of adults who are not their parents, interest in the influence of children's relationships with these nonparental adults has peaked. The research reported in the present volume is a reflection of that interest. For infants and preschool children, the interest arose in the 1960s from concern that time in child care would prevent or undermine secure parental attachments (see McCartney and Galanopoulos, 1988, for a review). Researchers of school-age children (kindergarten and older) have more recently begun to examine the effects of teacher-child relationships beyond the traditional "teaching effectiveness" paradigm (for example, Wubbels, Brekelmans, and Hooymayers, 1991), perhaps partially a reflection of a "trickle-up" effect of concerns originating in the early childhood literature.

A relevant issue for both of these two conceptually linked lines of research is continuity versus discontinuity of child-adult relationships for home and out-of-home settings. In other words, the extent to which parent-child and teacher-child relationships are similar or different and their joint impact on children's development are major interests. Several of the studies in this volume address the nature of continuity versus discontinuity of children's relationships with their parents versus nonparental adults (teachers or caregivers). The attachment framework is an excellent lens through which to view the issue of continuity and discontinuity of children's experiences. This is because attachment researchers have extended their interest in concordance of multiple attachment relationships to relationships with nonparental adults. The notion

NEW DIRECTIONS FOR CHILD DEVELOPMENT, no. 57, Fall 1992 © Jossey-Bass Publishers of concordance from an attachment perspective can easily be construed as continuity within an ecological framework.

Another underlying issue for these two lines of research is contextual factors that distinguish home, child care, and school settings, thus determining relevant questions asked and interpretations of data obtained in these two settings. One contribution of Bronfenbrenner's (1979a) ecological model is its dual focus on the characteristics of individuals and the contexts in which they live as interdependent influences on development. No longer is it acceptable to explain developmental processes by simply examining precursors at the individual level. Alternatively, Bronfenbrenner has provided a framework that divides environmental contexts into multiple levels according to their proximity to individuals (the micro-, exo-, and macrosystems). The impact of the ecological model is evident in the research presented in this volume. Continuity and discontinuity of children's relationships with parents and nonparental adults have been shown to be partially dependent on similarities and differences in the contexts within which those relationships take place. Attention to context helps us to discern predictable continuities and discontinuities that, based on individual characteristics alone, may seem unpredictable or inconsistent.

The purpose of this chapter is to review the research reported in this volume from an ecological perspective. In other words, results of these studies are examined for the light that they can shed on the issues of continuity and context as well as the relationship between the two.

Continuity Versus Discontinuity

Researchers and practitioners concerned with young children frequently stress the benefits of continuity of experience for optimal child development (Bronfenbrenner, 1979b; Peters and Kontos, 1987). It is assumed, so far without empirical evidence, that children are more likely to thrive when there is continuity rather than discontinuity between the home and classroom environments. In contrast, another strongly held belief is that, for certain children, discontinuity is advantageous and must be maintained to prevent developmental disadvantage. In other words, the assumption that continuity of experiences is always developmentally enhancing stands in stark contrast to prevailing beliefs that some children require discontinuity in order to thrive (Peters and Kontos, 1987).

The assumption that continuity is developmentally enhancing is comfortable if one also assumes that a child is securely attached or has an otherwise positive relationship with his or her parents or lives in a stimulating environment. The benefits of discontinuity are more attractive when considering children whose relationships with parents are less than optimal or who live in disadvantaged environments. Under these less desirable circumstances, the relationship of the child with a nonparental adult is less likely to be perceived as a complement and more as an antidote to the parental relationship. The most dramatic example of this is children who have been maltreated by their parents.

Peters and Kontos (1987) proposed that continuity and discontinuity be viewed as neither good nor bad but as neutral contexts within which development takes place. Evaluation of the developmental potential of a particular context requires, first, an assessment of the risks and opportunities for children in varying contexts against likely developmental outcomes for children. Thus, to the extent that a context enhances children's development, it represents an opportunity, and vice versa. By definition, then, both continuity and discontinuity may represent an opportunity or a risk, depending on the probable outcome for children. Hence, continuous or discontinuous attachment relationships for children with their mothers versus teachers may represent a risk or an opportunity.

Child Care Settings

Howes and Matheson (this volume) and Hamilton and Howes (this volume) directly address the continuity-discontinuity issue. Both chapters are concerned with the nature of differences between mother-child and caregiver-child attachments, assuming that differences are likely to exist. Earlier studies revealed that children's attachment relationships with their mothers and teachers were not necessarily concordant (Howes and Hamilton, 1991), but that children's relationships with their caregivers in some ways resembled those with their mothers (Hamilton and Howes, 1991). More specifically, teacher behaviors associated with varying attachment patterns (secure, ambivalent, avoidant) were consistent with predictions based on mother-child attachment theory and research. One difference, however, was in the intensity of childrens' relationships with mothers versus teachers. A cutoff score of .33 on the Waters and Deane (1985) Attachment Q-Set was used to separate secure from insecure attachments. The mean security score for children with mothers was .51, whereas for children with teachers it was .31. Thus, on average, children were typically insecurely attached to their teachers. In Hamilton and Howes (1991), the largest group of mother-secure children obtained an average security score of .67, whereas the largest group of teacher-secure children obtained an average security score of .33. If we use mother-child attachment as our standard for comparison, teacher-child attachment might be characterized as "barely there." The research of Howes and colleagues suggests that, regarding children's attachments to mothers versus teachers, there is a situation that might be characterized as both continuous (attachment patterns) and discontinuous (attachment intensity and concordance).

Hamilton and Howes (this volume) further examine attachment patterns for children with mothers versus teachers. By examining the differences within children's attachment relations with their mothers and with their teachers as opposed to the behaviors that typically discriminate attachment classifications, they unearthed another aspect of discontinuity between mother-child and teacher-child attachments. As Hamilton and Howes note, the marker behaviors discriminating attachment classifications between mothers and teachers were not the same. Their explanation for this discontinuity in relationships as well as the lack of concordance in children's attachment relationships—context—is discussed more in a subsequent section here.

The results of Van IJzendoorn, Sagi, and Lambermon (this volume) revealing the lack of concordance of Dutch and Israeli children's attachment relationships with mothers, fathers, and caregivers are consistent with Hamilton and Howes's results (and Howes and Hamilton, 1991) documenting the prevalence of discontinuity of children's relationships with parental and nonparental adults. Further consistency was found in the associations between the sensitivity of caregiver interactions with the child and later attachment security.

Van IJzendoorn, Sagi, and Lambermon developed three unique scales measuring the quality of the child's attachment networks: quality of maternal attachment, quality of family (maternal/paternal) attachment networks, and quality of extended (maternal/paternal/caregiver) attachment networks. Although the paucity of associations among these measures and children's developmental status in the Dutch sample cloud the conclusions that can be drawn, in the Israeli sample it was clear that family and extended attachment networks were much better predictors of children's developmental status than was the quality of attachment with the mother alone. These data seem to imply that discontinuity of attachment relationships is beneficial to the extent that it represents a compensatory function of secure relationships for insecure relationships. If the maternal attachment relationship is not primary, as the Israeli data suggest, then discontinuity of attachment relationships for children with insecure maternal attachments is beneficial. Moreover, even for children with secure attachments with their mothers, the fact that additional securely attached relationships with fathers and/or caregivers appear to be beneficial supports the claim of Van IJzendoorn, Sagi, and Lambermon that, for children with multiple attachment figures, the nature of the attachment "constellation" may be a decisive factor in children's later development. The integration model is thus a conceptually parsimonious way to address the continuity-discontinuity issue within the attachment framework.

The research reported here reveals both continuity and discontinuity of children's relationships with parental and nonparental adults that represent risks as well as opportunities for children. The fact that the majority of concordant (continuous) relationships were secure suggests that continuity of insecure relationships is not a major problem for young children in child care. That teacher-child attachments differ from mother-child attachments in intensity and form does not necessarily relegate the former to a lesser role (that is, Van IJzendoorn, Sagi, and Lambermon's hierarchical versus integrated models) or negate them as true attachment relationships. Rather, the discontinuity prevalent in these data collectively suggests that the attachment paradigm should be widened to include multiple parental and nonparental relationships and to take into account context, particularly now at a time when shared child rearing (even for infants and toddlers) between parents and other caregivers is the norm rather than the exception.

School Settings

One contribution of this volume is to stretch investigations of teacher-child relationships beyond child care contexts and into the public school context where such issues have much less frequently been a concern, either for researchers or practitioners. Research reported here suggests that these relationships should become a more salient part of our thinking about the impact of school on children. Recognition of the parallels (or continuity) between child care and school effects may be one way to advance our knowledge and practice in both domains (McCartney and Jordan, 1990).

Pianta and Steinberg (this volume) examine relationships between teachers and children through the eyes of the teacher. The STRS represents a unique attempt to conceptualize and measure affective relationships between school teachers and their students. The conceptualization was partially derived from attachment theory. As such, the associations that Pianta and Steinberg found between teacher-child relationships and childrens' behavior at home and school represent developmental continuity by revealing that the importance of children's relationships with nonparental adults does not end when children enter the public schools.

Issues revolving around school-age children's relationships with their teachers are a fertile area for investigation. By breaking away from the more traditional focus on teaching strategies and children's academic achievement, insights can be gained regarding adult-child social relationships in school settings and their impact on children's cognitive and social development. Pianta and Steinberg's results regarding differences in teacher-child relationships for retained and promoted kindergartners are consistent with the research of others suggesting that the basis for retention decisions is more than just academic achievement (Walsh, Ellwein, Eads, and Miller, 1991; Mantzicopoulos, Morrison, Hinshaw, and Carte, 1989). Do teachers develop stronger attachments to children who do well in school than to those who are struggling? Are the children who are struggling academically more difficult to develop attachments to because their academic difficulties are associated with less desirable classroom behavior? Would closer, less conflicted relationships between teachers and low-achievement kindergartners result in higher achievement and/or a better chance for promotion? These are questions that are only beginning to be asked by Pianta and colleagues and their answers will help us to determine the developmental continuity of the effects of nonparental adult relationships between preschool and elementary school.

Lynch and Cicchetti (this volume) investigated whether positive relationships with teachers might compensate for the negative relationships of maltreated children with their parents. Obviously, for this population, discontinuity of relationships between these children and their parents versus their teachers is desirable. Unfortunately, 38 percent of the children in Lynch and Cicchetti's study had concordant relationships with their mothers and their teachers. There was little evidence that teachers function as alternative attachment figures for school-age maltreated children. Lynch and Cicchetti suggest that maltreated children's negative representational models of relatedness based on their interactional histories with their parents may taint their ability to form positive, secure relationships with teachers. Thus, for maltreated children, a priority for practitioners may be to promote discontinuity of parent and teacher relationships because the developmental outcomes of continuity are known to be negative.

Research on teacher-child relationships in school settings is in its infancy. Consequently, there is less that can be said about continuity and discontinuity within this framework. Nonetheless, if we have learned anything about family and child care influences on preschool children it is that a variety of interrelated factors combine to produce their effects and these effects are moderated by child characteristics (McCartney and Jordan, 1990). Application of this ecological framework to school effects means that children's relationships with their teachers are one of many factors that must be taken into account in explaining children's development. It also means that we will have more opportunities to explore the impact of context on children's relationships with nonparental adults.

Context

It is clear that much of what has been discussed so far has had the aura of context hovering in the background. In this section, context is brought to the forefront.

Child Care. Howes and Matheson most explicitly address the issue of context via ecological-cultural theory that is superimposed on attachment theory in order to predict when concordance of mother-child and teacher-child attachment relationships will occur. The result is an alternative model, based on the activity setting approach of ecological-cultural theory, to the traditional hierarchical model posited by attachment theory that predicts continuity between mother-child and teacher-child attachments. The activity setting model accounts for nonconcordant relations among multiple attachment figures, particularly for children who enter child care prior to establishing attachment relationships with their mothers. Given the prevalence of nonconcordant attachment relationships for children with multiple attachment relationships, an alternative to the hierarchical model is a welcome addition to the attachment and child care literatures.

Hamilton and Howes also use an activity setting framework to distinguish between the home and child care contexts and, in turn, to predict differences in mother-child and teacher-child relationships. The differences between home and child care contexts to which they point (persons involved, belief systems of those people, emotional tones of the settings, competing tasks, and scripts governing various tasks such as feeding and playing) are neither esoteric nor obscure. By applying the activity setting framework, however, it is possible to transform rather obvious (and thus sometimes ignored) differences into theoretically meaningful predictors of children's social relationships.

Howes and Matheson and Hamilton and Howes have successfully employed the activity setting framework as a way to include context in predictions of continuities and discontinuities of children's relationships with the various significant adults in their lives. The results of both studies reported here were consistent with ecological-cultural theory in that degree of overlap between activity settings was associated with concordance in maternal and teacher attachments and, even within concordant relationships, differences in activity settings resulted in different behaviors distinguishing maternal and teacher attachments. Whether these discontinuities represent risks or opportunities is dependent on the particular combination of activity settings in which the child is developing. Belsky (1990) speculated that the negative effects of particular contexts on children's development are only likely when "sources of risk accumulate." Thus, the children from disorganized families who were enrolled in model child care centers and developed nonconcordant, compensatory attachments with their teachers (insecure with mother, secure with teacher) are likely to be better off in the long run than are the children with similar backgrounds who developed concordant ambivalent attachments with mothers and teachers. By viewing attachment relationships from a contextual perspective, these studies reinforce the notion that continuity and discontinuity are both potentially a risk or an opportunity.

Van IJzendoorn, Sagi, and Lambermon indirectly address the issue of context by using data sets gathered in the Netherlands and in Israel. Even though their prime intent was not to examine multiple caretaking from a cross-cultural perspective, differences in results from the two cultures generated a need to address cultural context issues by way of post hoc explanations. Based on Van IJzendoorn, Sagi, and Lambermon's description, it is probably safe to say that home environments in the Netherlands and the Israeli kibbutz represent different activity settings, as do the child care settings in these two contexts. If this is a safe assumption, then we might also assume that for comparable studies executed in these two countries, different results would be expected and similar results would probably have different meanings.

The results reported by Van IJzendoorn, Sagi, and Lambermon indeed reveal substantially different distributions across attachment classifications for the Dutch and Israeli samples, as well as different associations between network attachment security and children's developmental status. Insecure attachments among Dutch infants were more likely to be avoidant, whereas insecure attachments among Israeli infants were mostly ambivalent. The Dutch infants were being raised by middle-class dual-career parents in otherwise traditional Dutch homes. The Israeli infants, on the other hand, were being raised by middle-class dual-career families living in a communal setting that included communal sleeping arrangements for the children. Thus, the role of parents and caregivers in these children's lives and the circumstances in which they interacted with these attachment figures were different. In both cultures the majority of infants developed secure attachments with all the adults in their attachment networks, but the probability of an insecure attachment being avoidant or ambivalent was culture-specific. A more detailed analysis of differences in dual-career home and child care settings in Holland versus Israeli kibbutzim and how these settings are viewed by the cultures at large might result in explanations for the attachment classification differences that are compatible with the activity setting framework of ecological-cultural theory.

Likewise, an activity setting framework could explain differences in the associations between network attachment security and children's later development (assuming differences in methodology between the Dutch and Israeli samples can be minimized). It makes sense that, as the authors point out, the consequences of shared caregiving are more clearcut in a communal context and where the cultural climate is more favorable to dual-earner families and nonparental care. Due to its cross-cultural perspective, this study reveals in a way that the other studies could not how theories of children's development tend to be culture- (or context-) specific.

School. The school context has some similarities to center-based child care and numerous differences. The similarities include child-oriented classrooms for groups of children of similar ages and abilities within which children are placed for approximately a year. The differences include method of selection (schools are assigned whereas child care is selected), cost and funding (schools are supported by public funds and are supposed to be free of charge, unlike child care), staff turnover (higher in child care due to poorer salaries and working conditions), structural characteristics (group sizes and staff-child ratios are less advantageous in schools), programmatic goals and methods (schools are more narrowly didactic and achievement oriented than most child care programs), schedules (only child care programs schedule opening and closing times to accommodate working parents), and societal ambivalence regarding their roles (little for schools and significant for child care). Thus, the differences between schools and child care are many and substantial whereas the similarities tend to be fewer as well as more superficial. Attempts to characterize the nature and outcome of children's relationships with teachers in schools must be embedded in the unique characteristics of school contexts as opposed to "warmed-over" interpretations of research conducted in child care settings.

The school-based studies reported here are initial attempts to extend to school settings our interest in children's relationships with child care teachers. Although research with younger children suggests that multiple attachments may compensate for an insecure maternal attachment, Lynch and Cicchetti were unable to determine whether teachers can function as alternative attachment figures for maltreated children. Because their data suggested that maltreated children's representational models for relationships were based on their relationships with their mothers, they looked for limiting factors for teacher-child relationships both in the child and in the school environment. They targeted the limited time that children are assigned to a particular teacher as potentially inadequate for a child with negative relationship models to develop an intimate relationship. Other limiting contextual factors may be equally as inhibiting. For instance, the teacher-child ratio, didactic teaching strategies, and the emphasis on cognitive development may individually or collectively prevent teachers from developing supportive, compensatory relationships with the children who need them. Under what circumstances such relationships do arise is an important topic for future research.

Pianta and Steinberg targeted school adjustment among kindergartners as an outcome of teacher-child relationships. This is a different approach by virtue of examining variables other than risk factors in the home and the child and because teacher-child relationships in this study represent part of the school context rather than an outcome of it. By providing us with a "new angle" from which to view children's functioning in school, it is an important line of research. Ultimately, we must learn how teacher-child relationships are associated with other individual and school contextual factors and how they join with contextual factors in the home to influence school adjustment. An understanding of these interrelationships will help us to better understand the mechanisms by which adult-child relationships in schools influence children's learning and development whether these mechanisms resemble those for younger children in child care settings.

Conclusion

The research reported here documents how continuity and context in children's relationships are linked. It also helps to lay to rest the notion that discontinuity is necessarily a developmental disadvantage. The data suggest that for some children (although, perhaps, not those who are maltreated by their mothers) the maternal relationship does not necessarily form the basis for all other relationships with adults. While it is true that for preschool children, when continuity is present, both relationships are most often secure, contextual discontinuity is likely to result in discontinuity in relationships. Discontinuity under these circumstances, however, may mean that the secure relationship serves a compensatory function for the insecure relationship and thus is developmentally enhancing rather than disadvantageous.

We have much to learn about children's relationships with nonparental adults, especially in the school context. Models of children's parental relationships (namely, attachment theory) have served researchers well in formulating hypotheses about children's relationships with nonparental adults. The studies in this volume suggest that we should use these models as a framework rather than a template. New or revised models (for example, Howes and Matheson's addition of ecological-cultural theory to attachment theory) may be needed to explain differences in the intensity, form, and function of children's relationships with their teachers.

References

Belsky, J. "Parental and Nonparental Child Care and Children's Socioemotional Development: A Decade Review." *Journal of Marriage and the Family*, 1990, *52*, 885–903.

Bronfenbrenner, U. "Contexts of Childrearing: Problems and Prospects." *American Psychologist*, 1979a, *34*, 844–850.

Bronfenbrenner, U. *The Ecology of Human Development: Experiments by Nature and Design.* Cambridge, Mass.: Harvard University Press, 1979b.

Hamilton, C. E., and Howes, C. "A Comparison of Children's Relationships with Their Child Care Teachers and Parents." Paper presented at the biennial meeting of the Society for Research in Child Development, Seattle, Washington, April 1991.

Howes, C., and Hamilton, C. E. "Children's Attachments with Child Care Teachers: Stability and Concordance with Parental Attachments." Paper presented at the biennial meeting of the Society for Research in Child Development, Seattle, Washington, April 1991.

McCartney, K., and Galanopoulos, A. "Childcare and Attachment: A New Frontier the Second Time Around." *American Journal of Orthopsychiatry*, 1988, *58* (1), 16–24.

McCartney, K., and Jordan, E. "Parallels Between Research on Child Care and Research on School Effects." *Educational Researcher,* 1990, *19* (1), 21–27.

Mantzicopoulos, P., Morrison, D., Hinshaw, S., and Carte, E. "Nonpromotion in Kindergarten: The Role of Cognitive, Perceptual, Visual-Motor, Behavioral, Achievement, Socioeconomic, and Demographic Characteristics." *American Educational Research Journal,* 1989, *26,* 107–121.

Peters, D.,and Kontos, S. "Continuity and Discontinuity of Experience: An Intervention Perspective." In D. Peters and S. Kontos (eds.), *Continuity and Discontinuity of Experience in Child Care.* Vol. 2. Annual Advances in Applied Developmental Psychology. Norwood, N.J.: Ablex, 1987.

Walsh, D., Ellwein, M. C., Eads, G., and Miller, A. "Knocking on Kindergarten's Door: Who Gets In? Who's Kept Out?" *Early Childhood Research Quarterly,* 1991, *6,* 89–100.

Waters, E., and Deane, K. E. "The Attachment Q-Set." In I. Bretherton and E. Waters (eds.), *Growing Points of Attachment: Theory and Research.* Monographs of the Society for Research in Child Development, vol. 50, nos. 1–2 (serial no. 209). Chicago: University of Chicago Press, 1985.

Wubbels, T., Brekelmans, M., and Hooymayers, H. "Interpersonal Teacher Behavior in the Classroom." In B. Fraser and H. Walberg (eds.), *Educational Environments: Evaluation, Antecedents, and Consequences.* Oxford, England: Pergamon Press, 1991.

SUSAN KONTOS is associate professor in the Department of Child Development and Family Studies, Purdue University, West Lafayette, Indiana. She serves as associate editor of Early Childhood Research Quarterly *and* Child and Youth Care Forum. *Her research focuses on the joint effects of families and early childhood programs on young children and on early intervention. She is the author of a research monograph on family day care published by the National Association for the Education of Young Children.*

Research on child-teacher relationships has implications for theories of social development and applications in child care and school settings.

Conceptual and Methodological Issues in Research on Relationships Between Children and Nonparental Adults

Robert C. Pianta

In the Editor's Notes of this volume, I observed that each chapter addresses a set of basic questions: What dimensions best describe relationships between children and teachers? What types of continuity/coherence exist in relationships across people, contexts, roles, and time? How do children organize their experiences in these relationships despite the inevitable (and necessary) inconsistencies that occur (Urban, Carlson, Egeland, and Sroufe, 1991)? The chapters here address these questions using the best tools available; the research is based on attachment theory and research, and there are solid rationales for the methods and analytical approaches. Overall, the chapters provide evidence for a number of conclusions, each of which suggests directions for further research.

1. Children form relationships with teachers that, in many cases, are attachments and that have unique influences on their development.
2. Contextual variables related to the type of setting, intensity and frequency of experience with a teacher, and constraints on adult and child interaction in a particular setting (for example, home, school) affect the extent to which the child develops an attachment to a teacher and the quality of that attachment (or relationship).
3. Children internally organize their relationships with adults using representations based on prior developmental history and current

Preparation of this chapter was supported in part by the Commonwealth Center for the Education of Teachers, University of Virginia and James Madison University.

experiences. Representational systems are open systems with multiple possibilities for organization.

4. Global dimensions underlying teacher-child relationships (for example, emotional valence, engagement) are also present in parent-child relationships. The presence of common dimensions across relationships has implications for research on continuity.

5. Methodological issues, particularly those related to measurement, require considerable attention as research on child-teacher relationships moves ahead.

Child-Teacher Relationships and Attachments

It would be an oversimplification to view research on child-teacher relationships as answering the question of whether child-teacher relationships are "real" attachments. Bowlby (1969, 1980) observed that children show attachment behavior to a range of adults available to them in times of distress and may develop attachments to a number of individuals. By rather stringent criteria developed on Bowlby's definition of attachment behavior, Van IJzendoorn, Sagi, and Lambermon (this volume) provide evidence that children in child care form attachments to their caregivers in that setting; the Howes and Matheson (this volume) data support this conclusion.

Research on teacher-child relationships needs to take a broad view and not focus on attachment as equivalent to the entire relationship. That is, teacher-child (like parent-child) relationships serve multiple functions and are composed of multiple behavioral systems, or components, that are interrelated to some degree. Isolation of these relationship components, description of their interrelatedness, and identification of their significance for development constitute a broad-based agenda for research. The validity of child-teacher attachment can then be assessed within this framework, as just one component (behavioral system) within the child-teacher relationship.

Contextual analysis suggests that children have ample opportunities for activation of their attachment behavior systems when in the presence of nonparental caregivers (Howes and Matheson). The Lynch and Cicchetti data (this volume) indicate that psychological proximity seeking toward the teacher is prominent among elementary school children with insecure attachment histories; these children presumably desire contact, comfort, and closeness from their teachers. Young children frequently seek their teacher under conditions of distress: being hurt, isolated, sick, fearful, or anxious. Two sets of research questions follow: one involving description, the other development. Descriptive questions include the conditions (interpersonal and otherwise) under which attachment behavior toward a teacher (and other relationship components) occurs, the strategies used by children to mediate their experiences of attachment and the functions of teachers within these strategies, and the existence of stable individual differences in these strategies. The Lynch and Cicchetti data indicate that children's use of a teacher as an attachment figure may be mediated by prior developmental history, that is, nonmaltreated children reported less psychological proximity seeking for their teacher than did maltreated children. It is possible that a teacher becomes salient as an attachment figure when attachment issues have not been adequately resolved in other relationships. Furthermore, Hamilton and Howes (this volume) report differences in the ways in which attachment behavior toward teacher and parent are displayed and organized, intensity being one dimension of difference.

The second, developmentally oriented set of questions addressed in this volume includes the antecedents and consequences of individual differences in child-teacher attachment, the extent to which these individual differences lead to predictable outcomes (for example, secure base behavior) within the child-teacher relationship context, similarities and dissimilarities in antecedent and consequent conditions for teacher-child and parent-child attachments, and differential prediction of subsequent development from child-teacher and child-parent attachments.

Each of these descriptive and developmental questions can also be asked about child-teacher relationships in general (Pianta and Steinberg, this volume), or about components of the child-teacher relationship. It is critical that future research on child-teacher relationships not be limited to only the attachment component of the child-teacher relationship. Exploration, dependence, self-esteem, and attention may also fall within the child-teacher relationship, have considerable developmental importance, and warrant attention from researchers. Moreover, it is expected that salient child-teacher relationship components will change with time, as the function of the child-teacher relationship changes.

Contextual Influences on Concordance

The extent to which child-teacher relationships are attachments is not an either-or phenomenon but involves a complex set of interrelated questions. So it is with the question of concordance. Whether children show similar patterns of behavior on separation and reunion from mother and teacher is highly dependent on a large number of factors, several of which have been identified by Howes and Matheson and by Lynch and Cicchetti. Concordance can be unpacked into a set of questions involving the relative developmental significance of child-mother and child-teacher attachments within the child's representation of multiple attachments, and the relation between attachment and other components of child-adult relationships. Understood in this light, concordance data can be used to gain insight into critical issues related to continuity in relationships.

Several chapters in this volume suggest that children's experiences of their relationships with teachers are affected by their experiences with their mothers. Although these findings involve more than the attachment component of these relationships, they support the view that contextual conditions activate similar experiences for the child across relationships, and that the child's response to those conditions is predictable, in part, based on developmental history (Urban, Carlson, Egeland, and Sroufe, 1991). However, attachment research indicates that concordance within relationships across time, and across relationships, is not perfect (Fox, Kimmerly, and Shafer, 1991); development is open. Howes and Matheson suggest that concordance, even when found, may reflect (1) wholesale application of one representational model to a new adult (Sroufe and Fleeson, 1986; Urban, Carlson, Egeland, and Sroufe, 1991), usually accomplished in circumstances of high contextual similarity and predominance of the prior model and a secure history or (2) similarity in two independently acquired representational models. Howes and Matheson report cases in which concordance of the attachment component of child-mother and child-teacher relationships occurred under conditions in which the child spent extensive amounts of time in the nonhome setting receiving care similar to that received at home, in similar circumstances. In these conditions, the child may accrue sufficient repeated experiences such that attachment to the nonparental caregiver acquires equal weight (for routing developmental trajectories) to the attachment to the parent. In this sense, the relationship with nonparental caregiver functions in a manner similar to that of a protective factor or compensatory attachment in high-risk children (Lynch and Cicchetti), except that the child-teacher attachment is not inconsistent with the child-parent attachment. Thus, context can support concordant as well as discordant relationships, as described by Kontos (this volume).

Howes and Matheson identify a wide range of factors related to concordance. Type of setting, time in setting, adult characteristics (for example, attachment history of parents and teacher), developmental history of the child (across multiple domains), family and marital factors, gender (child and teacher), and ethnicity can all be expected to influence concordance. A detailed, microlevel analysis of classrooms and homes and of the demands within and across settings that can be expected to relate to attachment and other components of the child-adult relationship is necessary before an adequate understanding of concordance and discordance can be achieved. Such an analysis will require the integration of social development research and methods with ethnographic perspectives.

Organization of Representational Models of Relationships

Any study in which the child's experiences in two or more relationships are considered raises questions regarding the organization of the structures storing such experiences, and the processes governing their operation and function (Bretherton, 1990). Bowlby posited that children form internal working models of relationships in which are stored memories, beliefs, and postulates about self and other with respect to attachment. The concept of internal working models has been extended by Stern (1989) to content related to play, hunger, and other areas of relational experience. Most research on internal working models, or representational models, of relationships has been based on attachment data. When interest in attachment focused primarily on child-mother attachment, internal working models were thought to be based on child-mother experience; continuity with other relationships was viewed as the application of the model of self or other based on the experience of attachment to mother (Sroufe and Fleeson, 1986; Urban, Carlson, Egeland, and Sroufe, 1991). As interest in attachment to fathers increased, and data indicated discordant child-mother and child-father attachments, the challenge for attachment theorists was to determine how these disparate experiences were organized. Various ways of organizing two representational models have been suggested, each based on solid empirical data: sequential, hierarchical, and compensatory, with the suggestion that a model for any given attachment figure may itself be hierarchically composed of layered schemas of the self and other (Bretherton, 1990). Sequential and hierarchical patterns are similar in that both presume that there is a primary attachment figure (or model), based on sequence or salience of experience, and that the representational model of attachment based on experience with the primary attachment figure is dominant (Main, Kaplan, and Cassidy, 1985). Compensatory organizations are found in cases in which a once-dominant model has been replaced (or disconfirmed) through experience with a new attachment figure.

However, since data indicate that children form relationships with multiple adults, in many cases involving attachments, more complex means for studying children's representational models of attachments are needed. It is clear that comprehensive measures of the child's attachment experiences should include a measure of the organization of multiple representational models. Van IJzendoorn, Sagi, and Lambermon compared the predictive validity of several organizational patterns and found the best predictor, in one sample, to be a fairly global indicator of the child's experience of security within a network of caregivers, an organizational pattern involving information integrated across experiences with multiple caregivers. These data suggest that even the sensorimotor child encodes and stores information from various relationships in an open system of representational models, which, at the superordinate level, contains a generalized model of self and other (Main, Kaplan, and Cassidy, 1985) based on integration of experience.

The significance of research on child-teacher relationships for attachment theory and for theories of mental organization and representation is apparent. In daily life, the child encodes, stores, and organizes experiences from multiple relationships, several of which may involve attachment components of varying quality and intensity, as well as other components (for example, exploration, dependence, self-esteem) that vary in quality and salience. The extent to which prediction is increased, or coherence is understood and explained, will depend on the ability of researchers to develop paradigms for assessing the stage-salient representations of relationship components (Stern, 1989) and the defensive and integrating processes that govern the exchange of information from one to another. Stern (1989) and Bretherton (1990) suggest that relationship experience is encoded and stored by the infant (and with increasing sophistication and abstraction by the school-age child) according to the level of abstraction (lived moments, represented moments, represented scenarios; low-level versus general event schemas) and content (attachment, play, hunger). One could imagine a series of experimental situations designed to elicit encoded relationship information for different relationships, contexts, and content that would shed light on the internal structures used by the child and the degree to which the information from one structure was available to another (Main, Kaplan, and Cassidy, 1985).

Dimensions Underlying Child-Teacher and Child-Parent Relationships

Up to this point, this chapter has addressed primarily the implications of this volume for attachment theory. However, it has been emphasized that attachment is only one component of child-adult relationships for which concordance may be an issue; two chapters address aspects of child-adult relationships other than attachment. Children's feelings of relatedness to an adult, and adults' observations about and experiences of their relationships with children, are the foci of the Lynch and Cicchetti and Pianta and Steinberg chapters. Theoretically derived scales were used to assess child-adult relationships from different perspectives, and, in both cases, affective valence and degree of engagement were dimensions along which relationships could be distributed and patterned.

The cluster patterns from the Pianta and Steinberg teacher data are strikingly similar to the clusters observed in the Lynch and Cicchetti student data. In both studies, groups of disengaged (uninvolved), average (functional), and optimal (positively engaged) relationships were reported. In both studies, the valence of the respondents' affective experiences of the relationships (emotional quality, warm, close) and the degree of actual or experienced need for contact and closeness (psychological proximity seeking, dependence) were the foundations for these organizations. The fact that similar relationship patterns and dimensions were discovered independently for children and teachers in two samples using two different scales suggests the importance of these dimensions for relationship assessment and classification.

A number of studies report similar findings for parent-child relationships in terms of the importance of affective valence and engagement as global dimensions underlying relationship patterns (Anders, 1989). Together, the child-parent and child-teacher data suggest that affective experience and engagement or involvement in relation to an adult may be dimensions along which child-teacher and child-parent relationships can be compared for research on continuity and the processes involved in discordance. For example, self-reports from teachers, parents, and children on these dimensions may index movement from "insecure" to "secure" relationships and identify classroom factors associated with both positive and negative relationship outcomes for children. These data could have implications for teacher training, preventive interventions in schools, and educational policy concerning teacher-child ratios and programs for high-risk students.

Methodological Issues

The complexity of this research is apparent. Data are required on different relationships and contexts, child variables, and adult variables in order to more completely address the questions raised by the chapters in this volume. Yet, the tools available for measurement of these factors, especially relationships, are somewhat limited. Although the predominant methods within the attachment paradigm, the Strange Situation and the Attachment Q-Set, are validated assessments of child-parent attachment, with methods available for children of older ages (Main, Kaplan, and Cassidy, 1985), the applicability of these methods to teacher-child attachment and other components of child-adult relationships is open to question. Research on child-teacher attachment could benefit from the use of observational techniques such as the Strange Situation as long as classroom observation data exist for validity. Adaptations of the Waters and Deane (1985) Q-Set have proved useful and flexible in assessing child-teacher attachment (Howes and Matheson, this volume; Hamilton and Howes, this volume; Pianta and Nimetz, 1992), but they lack classroom validity data. Observational systems such as those developed by Sroufe and colleagues (for example, Urban, Carlson, Egeland, and Sroufe,

1991) are promising because they are based on records of actual interactive behaviors between child and teacher in the normal flow of behavior in the school setting. Currently, these systems involve components of the child-teacher relationship other than attachment per se (for example, dependence), but they enable testing of theoretically derived hypotheses about continuity across relationships and time (Urban, Carlson, Egeland, and Sroufe, 1991).

Lynch and Cicchetti argue that assessment of relationships, and their interrelated components, must involve multiple assessment from different perspectives across contexts and time. Hinde (1987) makes a similar argument and suggests that such complex assessments are prerequisite to capturing the systemic (versus individual) nature of relationships. Q-Set data provide major advantages for such an approach because of their global nature, but these data can be limited if not collected from multiple perspectives. The self-report instruments used by Lynch and Cicchetti and by Pianta and Steinberg, if combined in a single study, offer views of a relationship from multiple perspectives. Finally, future efforts to develop self-report and Q-Set methods need to differentiate among components of a particular relationship (for example, attachment versus play).

Conclusion

In sum, the chapters in this volume suggest numerous directions for future research that will undoubtedly have implications for developmental theories, research on attachment, and the development and utilization of relationship resources in child care and school settings. Integrative approaches to data collection (psychometric, ethnographic) and interpretation (theory, policy) will be needed in order to realize the full potential of this emerging line of research.

Suggestions for Further Reading

Barrett, M., and Trivett, J. *Attachment Behavior and the School Child.* London: Tavistock/Routledge & Kegan Paul, 1990.
This book is a rich description of interactions between children and teachers in the school setting. The observations reported provide information on the role and function of child-teacher relationships and their development across time. The book is compelling in its argument for the unique influence of child-teacher relationships.

Greenberg, M. T., Cicchetti, D., and Cummings, E. M. (eds.). *Attachment During the Preschool Years: Theory, Research, and Intervention.* Chicago: University of Chicago Press, 1990.
This volume contains work by leading experts in attachment research,

focusing on the preschool years. Chapters address issues of measurement and classification, continuity from infancy, organization of representational systems, and individual differences in risk and nonrisk groups. This book is essential as background for research on child-teacher relationships.

Newman, D., Griffin, P., and Cole, M. *The Construction Zone: Working for Cognitive Change in School.* New York: Cambridge University Press, 1989. This book is a finely detailed description of the process of teaching and instruction. It provides clear support for teaching as a social process and suggests a number of ways in which research on child-teacher and child-parent relationships can be linked with classroom instruction.

References

Anders, T. F. "Clinical Syndromes, Relationship Disturbances, and Their Assessment." In A. J. Sameroff and R. N. Emde (eds.), *Relationship Disturbances in Early Childhood: A Developmental Approach.* New York: Basic Books, 1989.

Bowlby, J. *Attachment and Loss.* Vol. 1: *Attachment.* New York: Basic Books, 1969.

Bowlby, J. *Attachment and Loss.* Vol. 3: *Loss, Sadness, and Depression.* New York: Basic Books, 1980.

Bretherton, I. "Open Communication and Internal Working Models: Their Role in the Development of Attachment Relationships." In R. A. Thompson (ed.), *Socioemotional Development.* Nebraska Symposia on Motivation, vol. 36. Lincoln: University of Nebraska Press, 1990.

Fox, N. A., Kimmerly, N. L., and Schafer, W. D. "Attachment to Mother/Attachment to Father: A Meta-Analysis." *Child Development,* 1991, 62, 210–225.

Hinde, R. *Individuals, Relationships, and Culture.* New York: Cambridge University Press, 1987.

Main, M., Kaplan, N., and Cassidy, J. "Security in Infancy, Childhood, and Adulthood: A Move to the Level of Representation." In I. Bretherton and E. Waters (eds.), *Growing Points of Attachment: Theory and Research.* Monographs of the Society for Research in Child Development, vol. 50, nos. 1–2 (serial no. 209). Chicago: University of Chicago Press, 1985.

Pianta, R. C., and Nimetz, S. L. "Continuity in Affect and Control Across Teacher-Child and Parent-Child Relationships." Unpublished manuscript, University of Virginia, 1992.

Sroufe, L. A., and Fleeson, J. "Attachment and the Construction of Relationships." In W. Hartup and Z. Rubin (eds.), *Relationships and Development.* Hillsdale, N.J.: Erlbaum, 1986.

Stern, D. N. "The Representation of Relational Patterns: Developmental Considerations." In A. J. Sameroff and R. N. Emde (eds.), *Relationship Disturbances in Early Childhood: A Developmental Approach.* New York: Basic Books, 1989.

Urban, J., Carlson, E., Egeland, B., and Sroufe, L. A. "Patterns of Individual Adaptation Across Childhood." *Development and Psychopathology,* 1991, 3, 445–460.

Waters, E., and Deane, K. E. "Defining and Assessing Individual Differences in Attachment Relationships: Q-Methodology and the Organization of Behavior in Infancy and Early Childhood." In I. Bretherton and E. Waters (eds.), *Growing Points of Attachment: Theory and Research.* Monographs of the Society for Research in Child Development, vol. 50, nos. 1–2 (serial no. 209). Chicago: University of Chicago Press, 1985.

ROBERT C. PIANTA is associate professor of school and clinical psychology, Curry School of Education, University of Virginia, Charlottesville.

INDEX

ORDERING INFORMATION

NEW DIRECTIONS FOR CHILD DEVELOPMENT is a series of paperback books that presents the latest research findings on all aspects of children's psychological development, including their cognitive, social, moral, and emotional growth. Books in the series are published quarterly in fall, winter, spring, and summer and are available for purchase by subscription as well as by single copy.

SUBSCRIPTIONS for 1992 cost $52.00 for individuals (a savings of 20 percent over single-copy prices) and $70.00 for institutions, agencies, and libraries. Please do not send institutional checks for personal subscriptions. Standing orders are accepted.

SINGLE COPIES cost $17.95 when payment accompanies order. (California, New Jersey, New York, and Washington, D.C., residents please include appropriate sales tax.) Billed orders will be charged postage and handling.

DISCOUNTS for quantity orders are available. Please write to the address below for information.

ALL ORDERS must include either the name of an individual or an official purchase order number. Please submit your order as follows:
    Subscriptions: specify series and year subscription is to begin
    Single copies: include individual title code (such as CD1

MAIL ALL ORDERS TO:
    Jossey-Bass Publishers
    350 Sansome Street
    San Francisco, California 94104

FOR SALES OUTSIDE OF THE UNITED STATES CONTACT:
    Maxwell Macmillan International Publishing Group
    866 Third Avenue
    New York, New York 10022

OTHER TITLES AVAILABLE IN THE
NEW DIRECTIONS FOR CHILD DEVELOPMENT SERIES
William Damon, Editor-in-Chief

U.S. Postal Service
STATEMENT OF OWNERSHIP, MANAGEMENT AND CIRCULATION
Required by 39 U.S.C. 3685

1A. Title of Publication	1B. PUBLICATION NO.	2. Date of Filing
NEW DIRECTIONS FOR CHILD DEVELOPMENT	4 9 4 - 0 9 0 0	10/16/92

3. Frequency of Issue	3A. No. of Issues Published Annually	3B. Annual Subscription Price
Quarterly	Four (4)	$52 (individual) $70 (institutional)

4. Complete Mailing Address of Known Office of Publication (Street, City, County, State and ZIP+4 Code) (Not printers)

350 Sansome Street, San Francisco, CA 94104-1310

5. Complete Mailing Address of the Headquarters or General Business Offices of the Publisher (Not printer)

(above address at 4.)

6. Full Names and Complete Mailing Address of Publisher, Editor, and Managing Editor (This item MUST NOT be blank)

Publisher (Name and Complete Mailing Address)

Jossey-Bass Inc., Publishers (above address at 4.)

Editor (Name and Complete Mailing Address)

William Damon, Department of Education, Box 1938, Brown University, Providence, Rhode Island, 02912

Managing Editor (Name and Complete Mailing Address)

Lynn Luckow, President, Jossey-Bass Inc., Publishers

7. Owner (If owned by a corporation, its name and address must be stated and also immediately thereunder the names and addresses of stockholders owning or holding 1 percent or more of total amount of stock. If not owned by a corporation, the names and addresses of the individual owners must be given. If owned by a partnership or other unincorporated firm, its name and address, as well as that of each individual must be given. If the publication is published by a nonprofit organization, its name and address must be stated.) (Item must be completed.)

Full Name	Complete Mailing Address
Maxwell Communications Corp., plc	Headington Hill Hall Oxford OX30BW U.K.

8. Known Bondholders, Mortgagees, and Other Security Holders Owning or Holding 1 Percent or More of Total Amount of Bonds, Mortgages or Other Securities (If there are none, so state)

Full Name	Complete Mailing Address
same as above at 7.	same as above at 7.

9. For Completion by Nonprofit Organizations Authorized To Mail at Special Rates (DMM Section 423.12 only)
The purpose, function, and nonprofit status of this organization and the exempt status for Federal income tax purposes (Check one)

(1) ☐ Has Not Changed During Preceding 12 Months	(2) ☐ Has Changed During Preceding 12 Months	(If changed, publisher must submit explanation of change with this statement.)

10.	Extent and Nature of Circulation (See instructions on reverse side)	Average No. Copies Each Issue During Preceding 12 Months	Actual No. Copies of Single Issue Published Nearest to Filing Date
A.	Total No. Copies (Net Press Run)	1200	1349
B.	Paid and/or Requested Circulation		
1.	Sales through dealers and carriers, street vendors and counter sales	84	74
2.	Mail Subscription (Paid and/or requested)	455	508
C.	Total Paid and/or Requested Circulation (Sum of 10B1 and 10B2)	539	582
D.	Free Distribution by Mail, Carrier or Other Means Samples, Complimentary, and Other Free Copies	76	146
E.	Total Distribution (Sum of C and D)	615	728
F.	Copies Not Distributed		
1.	Office use, left over, unaccounted, spoiled after printing	585	621
2.	Return from News Agents	-0-	-0-
G.	TOTAL (Sum of E, F1 and 2—should equal net press run shown in A)	1200	1349

11. I certify that the statements made by me above are correct and complete	Signature and Title of Editor, Publisher, Business Manager, or Owner Larry Ishii Vice-President

PS Form 3526, Feb. 1989 *(See instructions on reverse)*